Clarence Saunders & the Founding of

piggly wiggly

The Rise & Fall of a Memphis Maverick

···

MIKE FREEMAN

THE
History
PRESS

Published by The History Press
Charleston, SC 29403
www.historypress.net

First published 2011

Manufactured in the United States

ISBN 978.1.60949.285.4

Library of Congress Cataloging-in-Publication Data

Freeman, Mike, 1956-
Clarence Saunders and the founding of Piggly Wiggly : the rise and fall of a Memphis
maverick / Mike Freeman.
p. cm.
ISBN 978-1-60949-285-4
1. Sauders, Clarence, 1881-1953. 2. Piggly Wiggly (Firm) 3. Grocers--United States--
Biography. 4. Grocery trade--United States--History. 5. Supermarkets--United States--
History. 6. Self-service stores--United States--History. I. Title.
HD9321.95.S28F74 2011
381'.45641300973--dc22
2011012904

I dedicate my work to my family and friends who encouraged my effort. In 1980, I went to work at the Jefferson Square Restaurant. Located at 79 Jefferson in downtown Memphis, it was the site of the first Piggly Wiggly store. From that place came inspiration.

CONTENTS

Acknowledgements

1988, Thesis for the Master's

The author wishes to express his gratitude to Dr. Charles Crawford, chairman of his graduate committee, Dr. Berkely Kalin and Dr. F. Jack Hurley. The biography would have remained an unfinished idea without their instruction and editorial counsel. Dr. Crawford, more than anyone else, aided the author through many of the steps of research and writing. Mrs. Betty Williams of the Oral History Research Office deserves special recognition for her helpful advice. In 1987, the Department of History granted an endowment to the author for study at the Library of Congress and the Food Marketing Institute in Washington, D.C. The author gained valuable information with that endowment.

The author conducted most of his research at the Memphis Room of the Memphis and Shelby County Public Library and the John Brister Library of the Memphis State University. The staff at each institution gave to the author considerable assistance, especially Dr. John Harkins, in the early years of his research.

2011

So much has changed between then and now. Memphis State is now the University of Memphis. Its library is now the McWherter. Two of my professors have retired. Only Dr. Crawford, at this writing, still teaches and advises. I am proud to say that I kept in contact with many of the people who helped me then. They helped with countless other projects since, along with the additional work on this project. They have become my friends. I'd like to single out Patricia LaPointe and Dr. Jim Johnson, formerly of the Memphis Public Library, and Ed Frank of the Mississippi Valley Collections, McWherter Library. No one can do any research project on any subject in Memphis without the assistance of the people who operate those two institutions, then and now.

Other organizations helped me with the Saunders project that I should have recognized before. The Piggly Wiggly Corporation twice sent me to Jacksonville, Florida, to interview retired company officials. Piggly Wiggly also opened its archives of company literature. I would like to thank Larney Crane, then president of the company, Ed Matthews, Melissa Ingram and Danny Barnwell. The Memphis Pink Palace Museum has a vested interest in Saunders. In the annex building is the replica of the first Piggly Wiggly store, complete with the turnstiles and paper price tags. The Saunders family willed to the museum many of Clarence's antiques, which can be seen in the restored mansion. Thank you, Ron Brister, now retired, and the staff at the Pink Palace. Since 1988, many people have helped me in the revisions and additional research, most notably Frank Reuter of Berryville, Arkansas.

This project really did have its beginning in a bar. Owner Jake Schorr wanted me to find the history of the building we worked in, 79 Jefferson. He told me that this was where Saunders created Piggly Wiggly. I was thrilled. I thought I was inside the equivalent of Henry Ford's first machine shop or Edison's lab. Maybe Saunders doesn't rise to the level of those two. But I had my goal, my purpose for the day. And thanks to my friends Tim and Hema Warren for providing me housing and company on my one research visit to Washington, D.C.

Lastly, I want to thank Bill and the late Mary Freeman, my dad and mom. They gave me every support long after I was supposed to be self-supporting. Near the end of my thesis research, they bought their first computer, a Mac. My uncle, Thomas McCloskey, happened to be there and was able to show me how to "open" and "save" so that I could complete the first version of this document over twenty years ago. Thank all of you again for your help.

Chapter 1

WHOLESALE GROCERY DRUMMER

I was a perambulating course in retail merchandising.

Clarence Saunders was born on August 9, 1881, into a family of dreamers. His parents were Abram Warwick and Mary Gregory Saunders. Abram was forty-seven when Clarence was born and the father of five children. Mary, his second wife, was twenty-six. She died when Clarence was just five years old.

The Saunderses had owned a plantation in Amherst County, Virginia. Abram Saunders fought with Confederate general Stonewall Jackson during the Civil War. Like many southern families, he lost his wealth during the war and Reconstruction years. No doubt Abram's careless handling of money was partly responsible for the loss. Years later, Saunders remembered him as "a real, high flying Virginia gentleman who lived up everything he inherited by the time he was fifty. He never worried about money." For the 1880 census, Abram described himself as a "dealer in novelties." Precisely what he sold is unknown.

Clarence's half brother, Abram Warwick Jr., fared better than his namesake father. Warwick Saunders was eighteen when Clarence was born. He left Virginia with his wife for the West. Warwick operated weekly newspapers in Platte City and Columbus, Nebraska. He was a fearless crusader in his editorials. People he castigated often challenged him to fights in the streets. Warwick, in turn, was an eager brawler. He was not a successful businessman. The newspapers eventually failed, as did his publishing companies in Omaha, Nebraska, and Davenport, Iowa. Warwick often organized and promoted with little money of his own. He failed for two reasons, his son Harris later reasoned: Warwick often trusted the wrong people in his various partnerships and joint ventures, and laws of the day did not adequately protect the financially weak in business from the strong. Prosperity finally blessed Warwick's clan in 1916. That year, a momentous year for the Saunders family, son Josiah Ellis in Omaha founded one of the first auto leasing businesses in the country. The Saunders Leasing Corporation was prominent in the transportation leasing business through the 1960s.

In 1891, Abram Sr. moved his family to Montgomery County, Tennessee. He married again, to Lou Ella Saunders, who would bear him five additional children. For the one-time landowner, Abram's position was now an embarrassment. He was employed by the Corbindale Plantation as a common laborer and sharecropper. The plantation fronted the Cumberland River, west of the village of Palmyra, less than ten miles from the county seat, Clarksville. Nashville, the state capital, was fifty miles southeast. The plantation was three hundred acres of limestone hills and valleys in Middle Tennessee, suited for burley and dark fired tobacco, wheat and apples. The Corbin family sold tobacco, country hams and apples. The Louisville and Nashville Railroad crossed their property parallel to the river. The railroad operated a repair station on the plantation where Abram also worked as a carpenter.

The family lived inside a drafty old commissary store on the property. Winters were especially difficult, with young Clarence substituting burlap bags for shoes. His father once tried to buy shoes for Clarence but lacked the necessary credit. A neighbor, Mr. Sinks, bought the shoes for the boy. When he became rich, Clarence Saunders would repay him for that act of generosity with a $100 bill every Christmas. Clarence never forgot his sharecropping labor with his father: "Tobacco hills I have made by the thousands with the hoe as my daily companion, setting out tobacco plants till my back was nearly broken." He chopped wood and picked blackberries to sell in Clarksville. At age eleven, he worked in the summer at a nearby sawmill and then a limestone kiln. For eleven hours of labor, he earned twenty-five cents a day. His formal education was brief, consisting of less than two years at a schoolhouse in Palmyra. The children there made fun of his shabby appearance, taunting "the barefoot boy." Ashamed of his destitute circumstances, he learned from the schoolyard experiences "to regiment his feelings until nothing hurt him." Nevertheless, the rest of his life, Saunders remained sensitive to the laughter of others. He fought hard, physically or with the force of his temper, against those who mocked him or questioned his character.

During Christmas holidays, Saunders worked for Burl Owens's general store in Palmyra. Owens was also the village postmaster. One of Saunders's first jobs for Owens was to clean and oil the kerosene lamps. He resolved at nine years of age "to become the best wick trimmer and lamp cleaner of the whole village." When Saunders was fourteen, Owens offered him a permanent job at four dollars a month plus room and board. Saunders defied his father and quit school forever to take the job. He opened the store at five o'clock in the morning and closed it about ten o'clock in the evening. Owens thought so much of Saunders's work that he doubled his pay within six months. But Saunders left that job for a similar position at ten dollars a month in Cumberland City, a three-mile walk from home. The storekeeper in Cumberland City was also a rail station agent. Saunders applied himself to new and more complex tasks in tariffs and shipping rates. Then, at age seventeen, the restless young man went to Blossburg, Alabama, near Birmingham, where Warwick had moved. Clarence became a night watchman for 150 coke ovens in a steel mill for a dollar a day. He read books on the job, beginning a habit of self-education. Burl Owens offered him his old job back, this time for half of the profits of the store. Soon Owens sold the store, and Saunders had to seek new work. He landed a job with his brother Moir at a sawmill in Cumberland City for a dollar a day. Hard physical labor made young Saunders a very strong man, strong enough in his middle age to lift and carry a 185-pound National Cash Register. He was of average height, only five feet, nine inches. He was of stocky build, with broad shoulders and forearms "as large as wrestlers." Saunders was determined to break away from the drudgery of manual labor. He knew education was the key to self-improvement, and whenever possible, he read books of all types; Thackeray, American political philosophy and poetry were his favorites. He developed his skills in math to the point where he could add and subtract columns of numbers in his head.

At nineteen he found a job in the wholesale grocery business. John Hurst and Joseph Boillin, wholesale merchants in Clarksville, had noticed potential in Saunders, who not long before had sold them blackberries. They employed him as a bill clerk at thirty dollars a month. Saunders learned the business quickly, progressing from bill clerk to cost clerk. Three years later, his wages grew to ninety dollars a month. The young man felt like a "prince" on his salary and spent seventeen dollars a month on a boardinghouse, the finest in town. The young man also had some responsibility as a provider for his stepmother and siblings. Abram Saunders died July 17, 1903, at the age of seventy-six. The old man was buried in an unmarked grave.

It is not known when Saunders met Carolyn Amy Walker of McLeansboro, Illinois. She probably attended the Clarksville Female Academy. Carolyn was a tall, striking and prim Victorian woman. They appeared to be an unlikely match. Her father, Leonidas Walker, was a successful lawyer and elected official in Hamilton County, Illinois, in marked contrast to Clarence's downtrodden family. Indeed, Carolyn would have little in common with Clarence's relatives. But by showing initiative, Clarence had already risen above his humble status. Perhaps their mutual love for books drew them together. He wrote poetry for her. Clarence and Carolyn Saunders were married in her hometown on October 6, 1903.

The following year they moved to Memphis, Tennessee, for a promising new job for Clarence: salesman at Shanks, Phillips & Co., wholesale grocers, at eighty-five dollars a month. Memphis was the right town for a young man anxious to succeed in this trade. Located on the Mississippi River close to the midwestern states, Memphis was a natural point of exchange between the North and South, with railroads tying the city to areas not accessible by the river and its tributaries. The city was surrounded by fertile land devoted to cotton production. Early in its history, Memphis became the largest interior market for cotton in the nation. Cotton merchants, or factors, often sold large quantities of food products to their landowner clients, who in turn fed and housed farm laborers. After the Civil War and the yellow fever epidemics of the 1870s, Memphians created an economic boom. By the 1890s, city merchants ranked fifth in the nation in wholesale sales, a figure well out of proportion to the city's rank in population. Memphis merchants took advantage of railroad expansion and the construction of a bridge across the Mississippi to build their trade territory. Their salesmen traveled as far as East Texas in pursuit of clients. Saunders's new employers, Samuel Phillips and H.B. Shanks, had also prospered in the wholesale trade after the Civil War. They sold groceries in ten southern states. Their specialties were grain and flour.

By the turn of the century, the city's population had more than tripled, from 33,000 in 1880 to 102,000. The grocery business changed with this migration of southern people from the farm to the city. Fewer cotton merchants carried grocery products in stock as the functions of cotton factoring and wholesale trade began to separate. Wholesale merchants, often called jobbers, paid more attention to the city retail trade. The same merchants also sold more often to southern town merchants, as well as the old plantation commissaries.

The traveling salesman, or drummer, found great differences among the grocery shops he called upon. Still, all of his shopkeeper clients shared some common needs. An ordinary shopkeeper tempted customers from the street with an arrangement of placards and displays at the front window. Once inside, the customer saw clerks behind display counters, tables and maybe a glass cigar stand stocked with goods. The shoppers entered the store and expected to be waited upon by the storekeeper or his clerks. When they requested grocery items, the clerks would go to shelves in the rear of the store and find them, usually one at a time. If necessary, the clerk ground coffee or sliced and weighed cheese. Then he put all the items on the counter. When the customer's list was exhausted, the clerk would laboriously add it up, sometimes on the back of a paper sack or perhaps order blanks, depending on the class of store and its customers. He usually asked if the purchase was to be paid now or listed on a charge account. At last, he put the groceries in the sack, "thanking him profusely for the business."

The considerate grocer kept loyal customers with other services in addition to charge accounts. Some grocers sent clerks into neighborhoods soliciting orders. Daily shopping for perishable goods was a necessity for the housewife or servant, for home refrigeration was limited to a block of ice in a box. The grocer and housewife telephoned each other to place the day's order. The housewife did not have to enter the store. For an extra fee, she could have her order delivered to her home, often by a boy driving a team of horses or mules. Home deliveries eased the strain of daily shopping. "I don't expect you to come to my store," one grocer asserted in a business magazine. "Make your selections and carry home your purchases; the risk of spoiling a good dress is too great. We grocers are equipped to deliver groceries at a comparatively small expense."

Not all grocers were this decent. Many were as crudely unsanitary as a frontier trading post. Some grocers sold liquor or beer in the back of the store. These places were notorious for their boisterous clientele. Few grocers clearly marked their merchandise with price labels. The unscrupulous took advantage by charging higher prices to customers they did not know or like. Clerks often short-weighed measured items or mixed spoiled produce with the fresh in a customer's order. If customers tried to pick out the items themselves, the clerks said, "Let me help you," or "Take what is given you."

The merchandise that salesmen hawked to the shopkeeper was gradually changing. Manufacturers in food processing developed products more convenient for kitchen preparation. Already, industrial canning allowed families to eat fruits and vegetables out of season. No longer were people limited to a "winter diet" of meat, bread and potatoes. Canned or packaged food did not spoil as readily as unprocessed food sold in barrels or in large sacks. This packaging made it easier to handle commodities in the home. Canned coffee relieved store clerks and housewives from the task of grinding coffee beans. Manufacturers placed greater emphasis on the labels and package designs. Trademarked names and labels were displayed in newspaper and magazine advertisements. They wanted the grocers, and the shoppers, to see that trademark as a symbol of their product and of their dependable quality.

Saunders quickly made a reputation in his territory. Already Saunders had more than enough courage to approach a potential client. Years later, Saunders described the most important requirement of a salesman—to be absolutely convinced of the value of the product. "A salesman must have that enthusiasm," he once said, "but the enthusiasm must be in the firm belief in the thing sold, not an enthusiasm limited in the desire to sell." The worst approach a salesman could make to a customer was to appear desperate for a commission. Saunders also enjoyed making abrupt statements to customers: "I like to watch the expression of a man's face when I say something unexpected that catches him off his guard…It is only by being able to startle or surprise a person…that their true character is discovered."

He did not like small-volume orders, bluntly demanding that some grocers order more than $400 at a sales call or see another salesman. When questioned about prices, he responded, "I can beat this price here and skin you somewhere else." His employers received a few complaints similar to this one: "That young salesman, Saunders, was too perky and smart to suit me when he first entered the store." He explained to his bosses that he had to motivate the shopkeepers to buy. They realized the complaining grocers often placed big orders with him. Whatever he lacked in tact, he compensated with results. Within two years, Saunders was earning an income of $125 per month.

Typical for him, Saunders did not stay at this job for long. At some time he moved to Omaha, the home of Warwick's sons. There he worked for McCord-Brady wholesalers for an indefinite period of time before moving back to Tennessee.

In 1908, Saunders accepted a unique challenge by William Cole Early. His new employer sold groceries to one Memphis grocer, Duke Bowers. Bowers was not liked by Early's other shopkeeper customers because his efficient methods and reduced prices undermined their own market share. As long as Early sold to Bowers, his other city grocers refused to buy from him. Some manufacturers also refused to sell their products to Bowers, for he would not agree to sell the goods at their fixed price. In fact, the Bowers boycott became part of a national debate over the practice of price fixing in the grocery trade. Saunders was hired to break the shopkeepers' boycott. He would gain more from this job than a salesman's commission.

When Saunders called upon Early's former customers, he heard an angry tirade about his employer. Now, his blunt manner was a disadvantage. On sales calls, he learned to patiently watch his potential customers and judge when they were receptive to him. He was a sharply observant man and always fascinated with the myriad practices of the grocery men. Saunders often visited stores before calling upon the shopkeeper. In his first presentation, he would offer tactful, friendly advice on how to improve the business. Perhaps the cashier's desk could be moved elsewhere to relieve counter congestion, a popular item could be displayed differently to attract more sales or pans of ice could be used to keep green vegetables fresher. "I was a perambulating course in retail merchandising," Saunders later portrayed himself. Then he mentioned an item his company had for sale. If the grocer showed interest, he followed up with a more thorough sales call.

He would later credit himself for breaking the merchant boycott of Bowers. But credit should really be given to Bowers. Instead, Saunders was a student of Bowers's grocery store practices. It is unknown whether they ever actually conversed about the grocery trade. Yet Saunders, the observant salesman, could not avoid watching Bowers's remarkable success.

Bowers had moved to Memphis two years before Saunders did, in 1902. By the age of twenty-eight, Bowers had operated a successful grocery store in, and served a term as mayor of, his hometown, Columbus, Kentucky. Memphis promised a brighter future for this ambitious grocery man. Bowers brought with him an unusual business tactic—cash transactions in the grocery trade. He had extricated his business once from indebtedness and resolved never to fall in debt again. Fly and Hobson, wholesale merchants, helped him select a store in a poor neighborhood south of downtown. They offered to establish a line of credit. Bowers insisted on paying for his supplies with cash, all of $279. In turn, he sold his groceries for cash only. Profits after his first day of business were eight cents. Experienced grocery men laughed at Bowers and said he would fail. It was unheard of not to offer charge accounts for one's customers. How could a grocer expect to keep any customers without charge accounts?

Bowers was a frugal manager. By cutting the bookkeeping expenses of charge accounts and the inevitable unpaid debts, he lowered his costs of business. He bought his merchandise carefully. Then he gave to his shoppers the benefits of his lower costs, cutting prices a penny or two below his competitors. He charged a uniform markup of 14.2 percent, 10 percent of which covered the cost of doing business. In contrast, his competitors traditionally added as much as a 30 percent markup. They often marked some items below cost to entice shoppers, a practice called loss-leading, while setting other prices high. Bowers offered free delivery for purchases over five dollars; for lesser purchases, he charged a dollar. A Memphian recalled that young boys would run errands to the store for their mothers and spend the penny saved on candy or cheese and crackers. They called his store the "penny store."

His efficient methods worked. Bowers sold $41,000 of groceries in his first year and $99,205 the next. By his fourth year, 1906, his sales in eighteen stores approached half a million dollars. He inadvertently created a penny shortage in Memphis. Banks had to make a special request for more pennies.

Bowers had a penchant for creating attention for his business. He named his stores both the "Temples of Economy" and the "Mr. Bowers' Little Stores." In half- or full-page newspaper ads, he made readers aware of his business ideas. His trademark design was a white bulldog of strong build with a black patch over one eye. The dog was muzzled by a leather strap.

Saunders learned a lot from Bowers; many of his methods became standard in grocery store management. The Bowers chain even had a healthy effect on food sanitation. He sold more goods at a faster rate than his competitors, keeping fresher merchandise in stock. *Courtesy of the Memphis Room, Memphis Public Library and Information Center.*

Under the dog was a caption: "You won't get bit if you trade at Mr. Bowers." He staged contests and gave away odd prizes, including a goat. By offering his store managers half the profits of the store plus salary, he provided a generous challenge. Bowers attracted men like himself to help run the chain.

The boycott did not stop Bowers; by 1911, he owned thirty-seven stores. He dreamed of owning nine hundred stores in Memphis and other southern cities, but poor health forced him to sell the controlling interest of the chain to the same company that first assisted him, Fly and Hobson. His promising career was cut short. For an unknown reason, Bowers then wrote newspaper ads campaigning against capital punishment. He died at the age of forty-two on December 22, 1917.

Eventually, Clarence Saunders returned to Shanks, Phillips for a city sales position and a raise in salary. Intrigued by the advantages of the chain stores, he persuaded twenty-one of his retail customers to form a cooperative venture. In February 1913, they created the United Stores, Inc. Each grocer retained ownership of his store but gave to Saunders at Shanks, Phillips wholesale purchasing and advertising control. At first some of the grocers worried that Saunders might take advantage of them if they allowed him to purchase most of the goods. He assured them he was not going to raise his commission and would earn his profits from their increased sales. He was teaching simple economy of scale; greater purchasing leverage would grant lower costs per item and greater profits. The retailers also saved advertising expenses with their combined resources. Every United Stores had an identical storefront and color scheme: royal blue with white trimming. He instructed the grocers to accept cash only from customers and to pay for all purchases with cash. The cooperative scheme worked, and Saunders's volume of sales for his employers rose from $3,900 a month to $35,000.

In June 1914, Saunders helped open a new United Store, jointly owned by all the grocers. This was the flagship store of the cooperative, managed by Saunders himself. Located at 79 Jefferson Street in downtown Memphis, between Front and Main, Saunders deliberately placed the store in the midst of established competition. To the west along Front Street were the old cotton and wholesale merchants. East on Jefferson from Main to Second were several butcher shops and grocery stores that already enjoyed the patronage of the many downtown shoppers. To gain attention for the grand opening of his United Store, his newspaper ads had the headline, "Free! Free!" Shoppers that first day were given souvenirs and flowers.

The business was successful, yet he was not content. He tired of laboring for Shanks, Phillips and watching most of the profits from sales bypass him. One day in February 1915, he met Cliff Blackburn for lunch. They agreed to form a partnership, the Saunders-Blackburn Company. Blackburn was from rural eastern Arkansas and, like Saunders, was a self-taught man. He had climbed up the ranks of wholesale drummers, working for a variety of produce and grocery jobbers. Blackburn had the winning charm of a salesman, kind and jovial. His new partner approvingly called him a man with "a Chesterfieldian manner…a friend to all." Blackburn offered quite a contrast to his intense partner.

That month, Saunders wrote a series of ads announcing the new company. He made it clear that this wholesale firm was different from the average wholesale grocery and would cut wholesale costs down from 8 percent to 3 percent or less. It would employ fewer clerks and no drummers, saving payroll costs. It would sell on a cash-only basis to country merchants who operated their own stores on a cash basis. He pointed to the United Stores as an excellent example of well-run grocery stores. The Saunders-Blackburn Company was to handle all the purchasing of the United Stores, worth $750,000 in sales annually. By April, they had persuaded seventy-two businessmen to invest a total of $22,000 in the company. Among them were James L. McRee of the Stratton-Warren Hardware Co., Andrew Williams, Elmo Pullin and Austin Moore. The latter three were owners of individual United Stores. Williams had managed a Bowers store until Saunders recruited him to the cooperative venture.

The new company sold $2 million worth of food merchandise by the fall of 1915, exceeding Saunders's bold predictions. Yet some of the investors were concerned. They did not see a profit from these impressive sales figures. Saunders had committed his company to selling goods at prices lower than his competitors, lower than the manufacturers' suggested prices. Some of the manufacturers boycotted him, forcing him to acquire merchandise from the other local wholesalers at higher prices. He had to have the merchandise, but he was losing profit. Perhaps, the troubled investors reasoned, Saunders needed help managing the business, or as one observer narrated, "They saw that the steam engine named Saunders needed a governor." Saunders exploded, "This is my company! If you don't like it, get out! I'll buy your stock."

They worked out a compromise. The disgruntled stockholders owned $42,000 worth of stock. Saunders paid them 20 percent of their stock immediately with the obligation to purchase all of it by January 1916, a four-month period. Within that time, the company profits reached $60,000, but this income was held in escrow. Saunders could not use it to buy the stock back. As the deadline approached, it appeared he might lose control of his business to them. Undaunted, he turned to additional friends, among them Joseph Boillin, his former employer in Clarksville. He raised more than enough money to pay the stockholders their due.

What role Blackburn played in this feud is unknown. Blackburn, from all appearances, was the junior partner and was content to let Saunders direct events. Perhaps he was a negotiator between his partner and the unhappy investors. Saunders had won his first battle with investors who, he believed, sought to control his enterprise. His confidence was boundless, establishing a fateful pattern of behavior for the rest of his business career.

In little over a decade, he had risen from a beginning salesman to the principal owner of a sales company. He was capable of attracting investors for his ideas. His income provided his family with a large home on Peabody Avenue in the most fashionable residential area of the city. He was the father of three children: Lee, born in 1903; Clarence Jr. or Clay, born in 1909; and Amy Carolyn, born in 1912. He liked to read stories to his children and shared with his boys a love for new inventions. A nephew remembered the cackle and screech of their ham radio in the attic of the home.

Another man would have been content with this successful position. However, Saunders was not satisfied; something was missing for him.

At the same time, many people were dissatisfied with the high prices of food in grocery stores. Food prices had been steadily rising since 1890. The beginning of the World War in 1914 drove food prices higher and at a faster rate. Wheat and other food commodities were needed by Allied armies and refugees. Unscrupulous commodity speculators had profited from the need. Yet the greater problem seemed to come from inefficient retail operations, according to business researchers. Chain stores had lessened business expenses, but that was not enough to stop food prices from rising. How could improvements to this lingering problem be made?

An answer came by way of a train ride.

Chapter 2
AIN'T THAT A FUNNY NAME

Piggly Wiggly will be born, not with a silver spoon...

At the request of Bry's Department Store, Saunders made a visit to Terre Haute, Indiana, in late summer 1916 to study a grocery store rumored to have a new and unusual design. The department store wanted to open its own grocery, and perhaps the Indiana store had the right design. Saunders found the store busy enough, but there was nothing new or unusual for him. On the train ride back to Memphis, rolling on past small towns and farms like his boyhood home, Saunders dwelled upon the problems faced by those in retail grocery trade.

He identified the greatest problem as the inflation of payroll costs in order to retain many clerks and delivery boys. In slack hours, clerks often had little to do but horseplay and banter among themselves, sometimes ignoring the customers in the store. In busy hours, they were swamped with customers, unable to satisfy everyone. Customers rushed to the harried clerks like piglets in the barnyard reaching for their mother sow.

Lulled by the motion of the train, Saunders was inspired. The name—Piggly Wiggly. What an odd and unusual name it was. That harsh consonant followed by the liquid sound gave "Pigg-ly Wigg-ly" a rhythmic feel. It spoke of childlike joy. He may have fondly recalled a nursery rhyme from long ago: "Higgledy piggledy, my fat hen, She lays eggs for gentlemen." Or a story he read to his children. Howard Garis's "Uncle Wiggly's Bedtime Stories" was a syndicated feature in the *Memphis News Scimitar.*

Clarence Saunders had found a name so unique everyone would remember it and identify it with him. During the next two hours on the train, the design for a Piggly Wiggly grocery store took shape in his mind. At the same time, he decided not to share his plans with Bry's Department Store. He would make his concept work for himself.

In his observations, he noticed that shoppers often entered a store with a prepared list in hand or had called the grocer to place an order. These people, he reasoned, had not needed the help of a salesman to

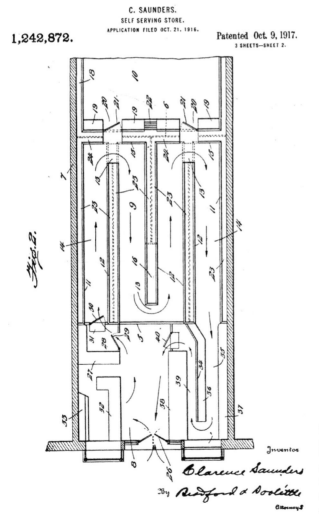

C. SAUNDERS.
SELF SERVING STORE.
APPLICATION FILED OCT. 21, 1916.

1,242,872.

Patented Oct. 9, 1917.
3 SHEETS—SHEET 2.

Saunders filed his first patent application on October 21, 1916. Patent #1,242,872 was granted October 9, 1917. *Courtesy of the Memphis Room, Memphis Public Library and Information Center.*

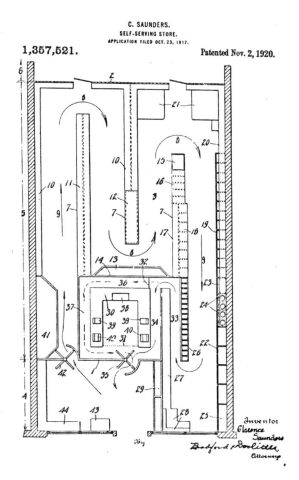

C. SAUNDERS.
SELF-SERVING STORE.
APPLICATION FILED OCT. 23, 1917.

1,357,521.

Patented Nov. 2, 1920.

One year after opening, Saunders filed three new patent applications to protect his new design revisions for the self-serving store. Patent #1,357,521 became the basic store design. The continuous aisle design is more visible. *Courtesy of the United States Patent Office.*

pick out their groceries. Why not arrange the store for those customers to do just that?

Back home, he hired the construction crew Semple and Lawrence to remove the old countertops and fixtures of his United Store at 79 Jefferson. Then they divided the 1,125-square-foot interior into three parts: the lobby, the middle salesroom and the rear stockroom. The salesroom was the largest of the three and the centerpiece of the innovation. In the middle of the store, the shopping area had cabinets arranged in a row to form a continuous path. At center left, customers entered the shopping area through this wooden gate. They walked the only path in view of items for sale. They chose their items to buy, which is "self-service." The continuous aisle passage led them through the store to a counter with a cash register at center right. After paying for their items, they exited the store through the gate attached to the counter. There was no space for a number of employees, and every item for sale was within easy reach of the shopper.

He stocked over one thousand different items of goods in his salesroom, approximately four times the variety of groceries in the ordinary store. Yet not all food products easily fit into his scheme and the available grocery store equipment. Most fruits, vegetables and meats required special attention to maintain their freshness and appearance. He decided not to sell fresh meats at first in the Piggly Wiggly.

As renovation neared completion at 79 Jefferson, Saunders began his promotion. Citizens of Memphis first discovered the mysterious name "Piggly Wiggly" on a billboard. After that another billboard read, "Mrs.

These photographs are arranged here in the sequence of the shopper's visit to show in detail Saunders's ideas. The front windows and the lobby of the store were devoid of signs, exhibit tables or anything that would clutter the view of his unusual designs. *Courtesy of the Library of Congress.*

Customers entered the sales floor through the left turnstile. The bin for shopping baskets was to the right. Here the photographer showed the cashier stand, adding machine and cash register. Saunders earned a patent for adding machine tape that gave shoppers a printed receipt. *Courtesy of the Library of Congress.*

Brown asked Mr. Brown to stop by the Piggly Wiggly on the way home." On Sunday, August 27, 1916, Saunders printed a quarter-page ad in the *Memphis Commercial Appeal*. In bold headline letter type, "Piggly Wiggly" commanded the readers' attention. Underneath he teased readers: "Will be born in a few days…not with a silver spoon in his mouth but with a work shirt on his back…When he arrives, you will be asked to call."

Already Saunders had targeted his advertising audience. Saunders "spoke" to the common men and women, praising their hard work and showing concern for their financial troubles. The Piggly Wiggly would work hard for them. It was a theme he would return to often, and he expressed his thoughts in odd ways. In his hand, Piggly Wiggly was never simply a store but a "person" who was "going to be raised on a scientific basis, with a scientific diet for each meal."

Piggly Wiggly was to be a business run on his frugal, efficient methods. Unlike any other store in Memphis, it would not offer delivery service, nor would it fill customer orders over the phone. Nor would it give away baskets; customers could buy a basket for three cents. He would fix uniform prices for all goods, whether sold by the item or by the pound. Commodities sold loose would be sold in uniform increments at the same price per pound. He would provide scales for customers to weigh their own purchases.

One week later, Saunders tossed to Sunday newspaper readers a half page of provocative statements: "Prices!! Go 'Way Honey and Sit Down. Believe me (the writer), there will be some prices at the Piggly Wiggly." Then he used the same tactic that had infuriated his clients at Shanks, Phillips a decade before: "Don't come though, unless you mean business and want to buy something. The Piggly Wiggly, unlike most fashion setting

The photographer has stopped at aisle one. To continue, he will follow the path of the sales floor to the end of the aisle, turn right and follow aisle two in reverse direction toward the front of the store. *Courtesy of the Library of Congress.*

The photographer has paused to examine one of the wall shelves. Shelves for grocery merchandise were attached to the cabinet spaces and to the walls. Saunders eliminated space for salesmen to stand among the shoppers. *Courtesy of the Library of Congress.*

patterns will be void of any sentiment." In the same ad, he softened his abrasive posture with a little self-directed humor:

> *Piggly Wiggly... Ain't That a Funny Name?*
> *The fellow that got up that name must have a screw loose somewheres.*
> *All this may be so, but the Piggly Wiggly knows its own business best*
> *and its business will be this: To have no store clerks gab and smirk while*
> *folks are standing around ten deep to get waited on. Every customer will*
> *be her own clerk, so if she wants to talk to a can of tomatoes and kill*
> *her time, all right and well—and it seems likely this will be a mighty*
> *lonesome chat.*

His ad poked fun at old-fashioned clerk service and stated the first commandment of self-service: customers would wait upon themselves.

His tenet implied that Piggly Wiggly employees would treat shoppers differently than before. Aware that the store design might confuse people, he later instructed his employees to watch for customers "looking about doubtfully as to what to do" and offer help. They were to direct shoppers to a particular item on the shelves when shoppers could not find it for themselves. But, Saunders decreed, they were not to pick up that item for the shopper unless the item was obviously heavy. They were not to suggest a particular item for sale or even imply that shoppers had to buy anything at all. They were never to coerce a shopper to take stale goods. Nor were they ever to negotiate prices directly with the customer. They were to treat everyone in a polite and courteous manner. His clerks were told not to favor their friends before other customers. Their conversation was to be limited to the business at hand.

The photographer has turned to walk the second aisle. The sunlight is apparent from the front windows. Notice the popular brand names of the canned vegetables and bottles of condiments. *Courtesy of the Library of Congress.*

Each grocery item also had a tag next to it, with a number clearly marked. The price tag was attached to a hook for his employees to alter prices efficiently. Saunders received U.S. patent #1,297,405 for his "Price Tagging Means" on March 18, 1919; filed on February 5, 1918. *Courtesy of the Library of Congress.*

Saunders would encourage his employees to follow his rules with sales incentives. They were paid salaries, from a salary allowance of 3 percent of the gross sales on the first $2,000 per week and 1½ percent on everything over that amount. After their salaries were met, what was left was distributed equally among them.

Next in his ad, Saunders bragged about the time-saving feature of his self-service store:

> *A customer wants five pounds of granulated sugar put up in a cloth bag.*
> *She is in a hurry, so she runs into the Piggly Wiggly and helps herself.*
> *She pays the cashier and away she goes. Another wants several articles,*
> *so she fills a basket, pays the cashier and off she goes. Every article in*
> *the Piggly Wiggly will be put up in convenient packages ready for sale.*

The refrigerator, which divided aisles two and three and was accessible from both sides, was attached to the wall. The self-locking doors kept butter and cheese cold and safe to consume. *Courtesy of the Library of Congress.*

He understood how seriously food price inflation had troubled his potential customers. The next day, Saunders wrote: "We are living in a fast age flow, in truth a little too fast. It is high time for some of us to put on the brakes and pause for a moment at the prospect of a downward plunge ahead of us in our reckless and extravagant living."

On September 5, he felt ready to show his new store: "The Piggly Wiggly Self-Serving System—a system that is going to revolutionize the retail grocery business." He announced that the grand opening of the Piggly Wiggly store was to be on the following day and would feature beauty contests. He shrewdly recruited the advertising managers from the three daily papers in Memphis for his contest judges.

Saunders promised his customers participation in another twentieth-century innovation. The beauty contest would be recorded by a "moving picture machine. If you want to see yourself in a moving picture, come

The photographer stopped in aisle three and looked toward the rear of the store. At the top of this wall was a footpath. Employees climbed a ladder in the stock room to reach this path and observe shoppers. *Courtesy of the Library of Congress.*

and get 'TOOK.' You will be able to see yourself right here at the Memphis picture shows." He reassured his female readers: "Nobody will 'make eyes' at you whether you are a contestant or not...Now, don't be timid about this. We are perfectly serious, and we do this to enliven things a little bit. Won't you help make our opening day a big success by entering into the spirit of the occasion?"

They came to see and be seen in the tiny store. He gave a flower to each lady and balloons to the children. A brass band entertained all. The judges awarded fifty dollars in gold to the contest winners. Red-haired ladies were their favorites. The grand opening was talk of the town that day.

The store visitors could hardly ignore it. Saunders designed the entire Piggly Wiggly store to catch the shoppers' attention. He painted the outside of the building blue, brown and yellow. Above the entrance, the words "Piggly Wiggly" beckoned in white letters on a blue background.

Saunders had placed bags of flour and other heavier items at aisle four near the end of the shoppers' journey. This photo also displayed his interior light fixtures, designed and positioned to illuminate two aisles. He obtained another patent for this design. *Courtesy of the Library of Congress.*

This section was next to the cashier stand, with shelving and bins for hardy fruits and vegetables. In his ads he called his produce bins the "Butterfly Wings of Piggly Wiggly." *Courtesy of the Library of Congress.*

Because the store renovation was not complete, he did not begin retail trade in the Piggly Wiggly for five more days, though he continued selling the virtues of self-service in his newspaper ads. In his ad "Green Hair, Blue Hair, Black Hair, Red Hair..." Saunders played upon his beauty contest. He said of his store, "A new standard is to be set in the distribution of food products economically...A store that has cut out all the frills of merchandising."

Apparently he had heard negative comments about his strange store, for he retorted in the ad, "So if some of you don't like our way you certainly will have no trouble in getting yourself pleased, provided you can be pleased (some people can't ever be pleased), as in Memphis there is every kind of grocery store to be found in the entire world."

Indeed, other grocery men laughed at Saunders when they heard of his arrangement of the Piggly Wiggly. No one in Memphis had seen anything like it. They said he was crazy. His new name suggested a "carnival house

Saunders had eliminated the flour barrel from the center of a grocery store. This machine in the stockroom sorted bulk commodity goods like flour into smaller pound packages. *Courtesy of the Library of Congress.*

for tots," not a business. There was no one to wait on customers, no one to carry the bags home for them. How could anyone keep loyal shoppers in a grocery store like that? That was the question Saunders's former partners at United Stores posed in their advertisement. Convenience in shopping, they said, was providing clerks to pick out and carry groceries for tired customers.

Grocers also feared they could not protect merchandise from shoplifters (a problem that still confronts retailers) if they had fewer clerks. Saunders admitted that he had not solved that problem. "By placing groceries in self-service fixtures, shoppers are then placed on their honor."

On September 11, 1916, he opened the doors of Piggly Wiggly for business. He had good news to report three days later: "487 customers actually bought goods from us on our first day." Changing his abrupt manner of his September 3 ad, he said, "Everybody is welcome to come whether they buy anything or not—prices plainly marked on each article." He also decided to drop the basket rental fee.

Saunders would answer his critics with at least a dozen ads over the next few weeks. He encouraged shoppers to try his new way: "It will be fashionable to save at Piggly Wiggly. Don't be behind time. Go to Piggly Wiggly and get yourself in style. People too snobbish to wait on themselves often take a summer vacation to escape bill collectors." Good service, he reminded them, is not what you offer but how well you perform. Grocery store service was not worth the cost if it was performed like this: "Your food at Piggly Wiggly is not dropped on the floor, knocked over by the clerks; not scattered all over the delivery wagon nor stepped on."

His customers, in contrast, received clean, sanitary groceries at prices "never seen before." He anticipated a higher volume would keep goods on the shelf fresh, in turn, pleasing his shoppers. Saunders was also meticulous about the cleanliness procedures his employees would follow.

On September 20, he told his readers of an incident in the store. When a woman was informed that she could find a pound of butter on aisle four, she refused to go there and pick it up herself. Instead, she walked across Jefferson into another store, bought her item and then retraced her steps to the Main Street streetcar. All because she refused to wait on herself; she had walked farther, had wasted more time and had paid more for her butter. "100 people can wait on themselves at Piggly Wiggly," he calculated in this ad, "every forty-eight seconds a customer leaves Piggly Wiggly with her purchase."

The Piggly Wiggly
'(Patent and Copyright Applied for)

His Ears Have Been Slashed--His Toes Cut Off--His Eyes 'Punched Out--His Bones Broken and His Face Smashed.

A Description of What Has Happened to the "DEMON of HIGH PRICES:"

Over his mutilated form stand scores and scores of mourners, who tear at their hair and bite their finger nails while they yearn for the days when the "DEMON OF HIGH PRICES" ruled with an iron grip on the hungry throats of the consumer who took from him, who had to sell a small portion for his money, whether or not he should have received from him a larger one.

Mourners of the dead, dry away your tears and if the grocery business doesn't look good to you any more, be happy that the consumer will now have a show and will henceforth from his throne at the Piggly Wiggly wield his scepter in the interest of his own stomach and his own pocketbook.

That which is good and better than the old no man should try to spill mud in its pathway. This time, though, mud or no mud, opposition or no opposition, the better thing is going to travel along its way providing for the consumer cleaner and lower priced articles of the same kind that have been and are now selling at higher prices in those stores still operating along old lines.

Every item is plainly marked. No clerks to argue with you, trying to persuade you into buying what you don't want to buy. You can wait on yourself in a hurry, or you can be as slow as you desire to be.

A basket is furnished FREE in which you may collect the different articles you desire to purchase—all packages wrapped FREE at the bundle wrapper's desk.

If you want to visit the Piggly Wiggly just to look through and see the system without buying anything, you will be welcome to call, and nobody will ask you why you didn't buy anything. A change in the checking system will be in effect Monday morning which will relieve the congestion that has sometimes resulted in the last aisle. Naturally some changes were expected to be made from the first start.

THIS NEW METHOD WILL MAKE IT POSSIBLE FOR YOU TO GET BY THE CHECKER'S DESK MUCH QUICKER AND WITHOUT ANY "JAMMING" OF FOLKS BEHIND YOU.

A newspaper columnist who knew him said newspapers were "a fine pulpit" for Clarence Saunders. "He liked to preach, the evangelical strain was strong in him as in most rural Americans brought up on protracted meetings, revivals." *Courtesy of the Memphis Room, Memphis Public Library and Information Center.*

Saunders continued to publish his statistics, his price lists and his sermons. In the story "Father to a Mother and Five Children," he wrote about a young, dirty paperboy who shopped at Piggly Wiggly. Someone thought the poor youth was going to steal. Saunders wondered why the downtrodden "innocents are marked with suspicion." His tale of suffering, inspired by his own hard childhood, was a reminder not to judge others falsely.

Three weeks later, Saunders opened his second store. The Latura family had for two generations operated a grocery at 633 Poplar, a neighborhood of merchant families and their antebellum homes. The Laturas' business, with fine crafted glass display cases, and their adjoining residence were considered quite elegant. Unfortunately, the heir of the family, "Wild Bill" Latura, was a troublemaker. The business closed after he was shot to death by a policeman. Saunders acquired the lease to the grocery building. On October 21, he opened the doors of "Piggly Wiggly Junior" to a waiting crowd.

The same day, he filed his first patent application with the United States Patent Office for his self-service store. In his patent application, Saunders never claimed to have created the idea of self-service; after all, the cafeteria, or self-service restaurant, already existed. Saunders predicted that his self-service design would be of great benefit to grocers and shoppers alike. He also asserted that his design was flexible enough to be adapted to other retail lines. The five and dime stores, he reasoned, could be arranged for self-service. Two witnesses signed the application along with him. One, Ernest Bradford, a Washington patent attorney, would have a long, fruitful association with Clarence Saunders.

Three months after the grand opening, he constructed a third store at 271 South Main. It was across from the new Chisca Hotel, close to the train stations and the warehouse district. He insisted everyone call his store "Piggly Wiggly the Third," not "Piggly Wiggly #3." It gave his stores "that royal dignity they are due." Wistfully, he talked of Piggly Wiggly stores opening all over the world, with forty-three stores here in Memphis. "One day people will be proud of Memphis because of Piggly Wiggly…And it shall be said by all men, kindred and tongues that the Piggly Wigglies shall multiply and replenish the earth with more and cleaner things to eat." On storefronts and letterheads, Saunders inscribed the phrase "All Over the World" just beneath the Piggly Wiggly name.

As he opened each new store, Saunders created new ads. In December, he began promoting Piggly Wiggly the Fourth. He had the gift of making literary characters seem alive. On New Year's Eve 1916, the character in his advertisement was a woman, a typical housewife, who had only three dollars for the weekly grocery shopping. She heard a friend talk about the new store in town, the Piggly Wiggly, and about its cheap prices. She was interested in trying the new store, but she had traded with one grocer for a long time and was reluctant to stop trading with him. The grocer had treated her well: "I thought about the kind face of my regular grocery man and how much he seemed to appreciate my orders. I also thought about the great difference in prices that appeared to me as I compared the prices paid by me to the kind-faced grocery man to the prices paid by my lady friend at the Piggly Wiggly."

Here Saunders had set forth the theme of the story. The shopper was beset with two conflicting virtues: sentimental attachment and the desire to save money. The struggle for her was to decide between the two, between the one virtue represented by the old grocer and the other represented by the new Piggly Wiggly. Then the lady said: "Now away back many years there had been a Dutch grandmother of mine who had been thrifty. The spirit of that old grandmother asserted itself just then within me and said to me, 'Business is business and charity and alms are another.'"

She made her decision and shopped at a Piggly Wiggly store. At the end of the trip, she still had sixty-five cents left from her budget. That was enough money to take in a picture show and put away fifty cents for next week's shopping.

Saunders had posed a question to his readers: given a choice between the old and familiar and something unknown, yet possibly advantageous, which would they choose? Saunders was convinced they would try the new.

Chapter 3
PATRIOTIC STORE

Piggly Wiggly...One in every neighborhood is sure to please.

By March 1917, Saunders operated six stores, which had sold $240,000 of groceries. King Piggly Wiggly alone sold $114,000. Obviously, many shoppers had tried the new. Saunders had demonstrated a chain store principle: opening new stores seemed to increase the business of all stores.

He compared the sales figures of his King Piggly Wiggly with the previous United Store. Operating out of the same building with almost the same clerks and management, the King Piggly Wiggly saved $1,800 in management costs and increased sales by $80,000. With self-service, he had reduced the cost of doing business from 15 percent to 4.

Saunders happily published most of this sales data in his grand opening advertisement for the seventh store. Piggly Wiggly sales for the week of March 29, 1917, were $19,000. From this data, Saunders projected yearly sales of $1 million and a profit of $35,000 based on 7½ percent markup over wholesale costs. He wanted to increase his capital stock from $25,000 to $100,000 by offering shares of Piggly Wiggly at $100. He enticed potential investors, "The biggest thing that has appeared in the merchandise world before...Ten years from now many folks there will be who will say to themselves, I had a golden opportunity to buy some of that stock." He promised this investment would build twenty stores in Memphis and a bakery with sales of $3 million a year.

The United States declared war on Germany on April 6, 1917. The Great War, now in its third year, profoundly affected Saunders. The United States Food Administration, organized under the direction of Herbert Hoover, set voluntary price guidelines for the wholesale and retail food trade to prevent abuses by unscrupulous speculators profiting from commodity shortages. Hoover would later call for voluntary rationing, "meatless Tuesdays, porkless Thursdays, wheatless Mondays and Wednesdays." President Woodrow Wilson created the Committee of Public Information, the first advertising campaign by the American government. On May 27, 1917, one week after President Wilson called for the Selective Service draft to begin, Saunders wrote an advertisement on the wartime problems with food distribution. He captured the patriotic spirit of the time:

PIGGLY WIGGLY

(Trade Mark, Copyright 1917 by Clarence Saunders)

War-Time Living With the Parasite! The Speculator! The Hoarder!

These two personages we do not need in our list. The Speculator is the man who tries to corner market by getting his hands on as much of a gle or several commodities as he may have, money buy, and after doing this, placing a much higher or itious value on what he has purchased than was a price he paid, knowing while doing this that ner or later the very need of the consumer will require that the consumer pay the price asked by him, are that the consumer will go without.

The Hoarder of either money or foods is he who as up for his exclusive use an amount of money or antity of foods in excess of his legitimate and rmal needs.

Neither of these personages have the proper conotion of their duty as it concerns others besides mselves.

Shall the blood money of the Speculator be piled higher and higher, while the hunger of the nation grows more acute every day? Shall each dollar extracted from the misery of the poor by speculation and hoarding be called a well-earned dollar? Rather, we should call such dollars "FLESH MONEY." Money carved from the unfilled stomachs of them who received only half rations, whereas they were entitled to a full dinner pail.

Shall patriotism be only the kind heard to the time of martial music, or shall it be the kind, whether on battlefield or at home, that will lay hold upon our hearts and hold fast there, excluding from the atmosphere found about our hearts—Selfishness—that mighty tyrant of wrongful living? The Speculator is selfish and so is the Hoarder. Throw them overboard! Do away with them! Place them outside the pale of the public conscience. Public sentiment will dry them

up 'till they will be consumed by the very selfishness of their souls.

To Arms, Ye Free Sons and Daughters of Liberty!

You who are best qualified, the rifle for yours—the plow for others—doctoring the sick and lame for some—the manufacturing plant for others—the mines for some—assembling and distributing the various products of the land for others, and governmental authority and work for some, and for all a unity of purpose in doing the best that he can in whatever patriotic endeavor in which he may be engaged, remembering always, " 'Tis for my country as well as for myself that I labor and do what is best for me to do."

Real Business Is Meant By Us—A Reading of the Prices Quoted Below Will Convince the Most Skeptical

Chief Special Patent Flour, 24-lb. sack......$1.63	Lima Beans, Soaked, No. 2 can......9c
Chief Special Patent Flour, 12-lb. sack....... .83	California Red Beans, No. 2 can......9c
Chief Special Patent Flour, 6-lb. sack....... .42	California Dry Lima Beans, per lb......17c
Snow Like Paper Patent Flour, 24 lb. sack 1.53	California Black Eye Peas 11 1-2c

Saunders also announced the first Piggly Wiggly store in another city, Houston, Texas. Saunders delighted in proving his detractors wrong: "Memphis will become famous as the home of the Piggly Wiggly. Now laugh you boob!" *Courtesy of Special Collections, McWherter Library, University of Memphis.*

He also announced the King Piggly Wiggly would move to a Main Street location. The Jefferson Avenue store was too small for the number of customers who shopped there. From the first month, Saunders heard complaints of congestion around the check stand area. Admitting that his design was flawed, Saunders, on June 3, announced a contest. He would award twenty dollars in gold for the best suggestion to improve Piggly Wiggly and five dollars in gold for second place. Then he cleverly asked, "Do you think Piggly Wiggly is all right?" He announced in the last part of the advertisement a second contest: "These are to be complimentary essays to take the bite out of the letters that tell us our shortcomings."

Saunders placed in the new King Piggly Wiggly other special innovations to his patented store. He replaced the entrance and exit swinging gates with two wooden turnstiles that expedited customer traffic in and out of the salesroom. The turnstiles allowed a less obstructed view of the store and were more open and inviting, providing an added psychological benefit. He also created a three-counter check stand with enough space in the middle for as many clerks. At peak hours, the clerks now could direct customers through multiple lines. Saunders filed his second patent application on June 20 to include the turnstile, the enlarged check stand area and the other improvements in the salesroom.

In his advertisement "Social Event of the Season," he extended a proper, royal invitation to visit King Piggly Wiggly in the new home. Only women were allowed in the store for his beauty contest. Everyone received a rose or carnation. Music was provided by a string band. The winners of the store improvements and the "Why Piggly Wiggly Is All Right" contest received their gold prizes. He published the best essays in the advertisement. One contestant, Mrs. Harry Jay, had praised him in verse:

When Piggly Wiggly came to town
We all looked with a kind of frown
We didn't think it could ever succeed
We didn't think it would amend our need...
So the greatest improvement that there can be
In the Piggly Wiggly system I can see
Is to give us more of them just like these
One in every neighborhood is sure to please.

The shoppers crowded in a Piggly Wiggly, circa 1917. He boasted in an advertisement, "100 customers can wait on themselves in the Piggly Wiggly, every 48 seconds a customer leaves Piggly Wiggly with her purchase." *Courtesy of the Library of Congress.*

No doubt Saunders was quite pleased.

On June 26, 1917, United States troops arrived in France. Saunders wrote a fundraising advertisement for the First Tennessee Field Artillery Battery A, avoiding, for the most part, the current patriotic hatred for the Germans. Instead, he pondered the fate of young men sent to war: "Sacrifice? Yes, Blood Sacrifice! Liberty calls for men to offer themselves as a sacrifice for her and yet does not deny them the prayer that the cup of death may pass by their lips. For some, the cup must be drank to the last dregs. For some it shall pass them by."

Saunders used his rhetoric to advance another cause most dear to him—preventing manufacturers and wholesalers from fixing retail prices. Cudahy Company, a wholesale supplier with a substantial business in Memphis, lost a judgment of $7,000 for price fixing. Colgate & Company, a manufacturer of soap, was indicted in federal court over this issue, though the company won its case in the Supreme Court. Saunders wrote,

"Show this New York crowd, that Colgate & Company can't dictate to a free citizenship in this city, at least, what they will pay for a bar of soap [Octagon soap]…the very idea of a soap man trying to be so mighty in his attitude toward the public. We may be a small potato, but we are not rotten and don't believe in evil ways."

Saunders instructed everyone involved with Piggly Wiggly not to trade with either company or with anyone who attempted to force a certain retail price on a product. He also forbade the use of trading stamps, premiums, manufacturer's coupons or any tactics that he considered to mislead shoppers into believing they were getting "something for nothing." He reasoned that if a company could give the product at a price with a gimmick, they could give the same price to everyone, all of the time.

Saunders began a publicity campaign against the Stevens-Ashurst bill. This legislation, pending in Congress, would have given manufacturers the right to dictate the resale price of their products. He wrote letters to legislators demanding their opinion of the bill. In a double-page advertisement, Saunders printed their replies, adding his own salty comments about those congressmen and senators who refused to reveal their opinions.

At the same time, Cliff Blackburn left the Saunders-Blackburn partnership for a sales position with a cotton brokerage firm. Neither disclosed why Blackburn quit Piggly Wiggly at a most fateful moment. Saunders wrote a generous tribute to Blackburn in an advertisement. They remained friends for many years.

Saunders published more sales statistics at the anniversary of the grand opening. In the week prior to September 18, 33,986 customers shopped at nine Piggly Wiggly stores. They purchased $25,755 of merchandise. At that rate, he projected annual sales of $1,339,253 and the number of customers at 1,767,272. The average sale per customer was $0.75. Piggly Wiggly stores in the city had an average daily sales of $510.45, except for the Binghampton suburban store with sales of $200.00. Average daily sales of the stores combined were $4,083.52. He offered a reward to any competitor who could outperform his sales at the nine Piggly Wigglies in Memphis. Saunders boasted that not even the Bowers Stores, with forty-three carefully managed units, could sell more groceries than his nine Piggly Wigglies. He had surpassed the Bowers stores in his first year of operation.

One month later, on October 9, 1917, the Patent Office granted Saunders his first patent for his self-service store. Within a month, he filed his third patent application. The store arrangements for the second and third designs were nearly identical, except that the fixtures and equipment in the third were portable. In his fourth patent application for the self-service store, he constructed two arrangements of fixtures and equipment. Both had turnstiles, but the continuous aisle designs were simpler than the previous self-service store patents. The store designs would carry less merchandise but would allow quicker access through the sales floor. He intended with his variety of designs to expand Piggly Wiggly into virtually any storefront, even a small booth within a department store. The Piggly Wigglies could be tailored in their construction to the specifications of a building and quickly installed. Saunders had in mind a rapid expansion of his stores. By the end of the year, he had hired forty people to build his store interiors and fixtures in a warehouse at 461 South Front Street.

In his fourth patent, he constructed two arrangements of fixtures and equipment designed for smaller storefronts, even a small booth within a department store. *Courtesy of the Memphis Room, Memphis Public Library.*

Eventually, he filed many applications for patents covering other specific improvements in his system: the price tags, the adding machine tape and the design of the interior electric lights. The patents and applications offered a variety of advantages in his retail grocery business. Protection from imitators was one advantage. The patents allowed him to claim a unique design, a particular advantage in salesmanship and advertising. The patents also helped create a standard of operations that other businessmen who purchased a license could operate themselves.

Saunders had refrained from selling his Piggly Wiggly idea outside of Memphis until he eliminated defects in his design. Now that the task was accomplished, he expanded Piggly Wiggly through franchising. He sold interested businessmen a license to operate his self-service grocery store. The Houston Piggly Wiggly store was merely a test to see if Piggly Wiggly could sell in a city where Saunders wasn't known. The King Piggly Wiggly in that city did quite well and so did the new Junior store, proof to him that his self-service stores could sell in any city. Kessler and Dixon, Houston grocers, were so impressed that they closed their store and remodeled it for the third Piggly Wiggly store. Other grocery companies were not sure if Saunders's ideas would work. The second-largest grocery company in the nation, Kroger Company of Cincinnati, had earlier sent a representative to investigate Piggly Wiggly. He produced a negative report.

To obtain franchises, Saunders wrote brochures extolling the virtues of Piggly Wiggly in his unique style. In a brochure written near the holiday season, Saunders could not resist mixing his business presentation with

THE INSIDE OF THINGS

COPYRIGHT 1917, BY CLARENCE SAUNDERS

In this pamphlet, he stated that grocers could increase sales and offer a return on their investment on just a 3 percent net profit. *Courtesy of the Memphis Room, Memphis Library and Information System.*

a little Christmas spirit. Saunders printed a standard Piggly Wiggly trademark contract for "Kris Kringle" of Nome, Alaska. Witnesses for the party of the second part were "Evergreen Holly" and "Polar Mistletoe."

The "Piggly Wiggly System" described his patented store designs, his merchandising theories and his expectations from franchisees. Franchisees paid Saunders an advance fee roughly equal to one cent per thousand people in the assigned territory, with a minimum fee of $500 and a royalty of ½ of 1 percent of sales, for use of the patent and trademarks of the Piggly Wiggly system.

This sliding scale fee allowed the small-town merchant to invest in Piggly Wiggly as easily as the city businessman. Saunders believed even the grocery man in a village of 1,900 people, too small to attract other chain store companies, could operate a Piggly Wiggly store under the proper circumstances. He asked small-town investors to observe his profitable store in Binghampton, a suburb of Memphis with only 1,200 people.

Each store had the same color scheme on the inside and exterior. The image here shows the exterior color design, the store name and the phrase "All Over the World" prominently displayed. *Courtesy of Alabama Department of Archives and History, Montgomery, Alabama.*

Small-town grocers proved to be among the most successful licensee holders of Piggly Wiggly. King Rogers of Dyersburg, Tennessee, bought his first Piggly Wiggly franchise in 1918 and opened a second store in 1925. The Rogers family would keep their franchise for more than sixty years. "Hallelujah! Triplets at Last! The royal princess and two brothers will be born the same day (January 14)," began his first Piggly Wiggly ad in 1918. Saunders opened three stores at once in Memphis. Everyone would know about this wonderful event, including Teddy Roosevelt. Saunders promised to send Teddy a telegram. He also announced his new endorsement of women's emancipation by way of "christening Princess Piggly Wiggly."

The demand for store fixtures—five stores opened during the week of March 6—had outpaced the production of Saunders's small factory. He and investors established the Saunders Manufacturing Company in Jackson, Tennessee. Isaac Tigrett of Jackson, James L. McRee, J.P. Norfleet and John W. Farley invested $50,000 for this larger manufacturing plant.

"Uncle Sam" holds in his outstretched hand a Piggly Wiggly store. Hoover said, "Every unnecessary service in connection with the distribution of food must be eliminated…in order that the people may have food at prices within their reach." *Courtesy of Special Collections, McWherter Library, University of Memphis.*

Piggly Wiggly's novelty attracted the attention of the United States Food Administration. The agency, in its *Weekly Bulletin*, commended the Piggly Wiggly system for helping ease wartime manpower and price inflation problems. Saunders proudly reprinted the citation in his ad on April 5, 1918, including a quote from Hoover. This official statement was proof to Clarence Saunders that he had accomplished a great deed. Piggly Wiggly will cut prices, he declared, as more people buy from Piggly Wiggly. He would honor all Food Administration guidelines, such as not advertising prices for flour and sugar. He did tout his special "War Winner Mixture," a combination of corn flour and wheat flour. It was a self-rising flour, perfect for biscuits, and if the customers did not like it, they could get their money back. Mixtures like this were substituted for the scarce wheat flour. "Wait on yourself with your own hands," he insisted. "Act like the store belongs to you, as it does belong to you."

Saunders again pushed his business toward national prominence. He formed a new partnership with Leslie Martin Stratton in June. He undoubtedly knew Stratton quite well. Both grew up under similar hardships in middle Tennessee; Stratton was from Lebanon. Both quit

Collier's magazine published Saunders's first national advertisement in the May 15, 1918 issue. He urged *Collier's* female readers to tear out the ad and send it to "your mother, your daughter, your girl chum of old days." *Courtesy of Alabama Department of Archives and History, Montgomery, Alabama.*

school to support family at an early age. Stratton came to Memphis in 1900 at the age of nineteen and worked a sales job for Cudahy Packing Company. In 1905, he founded his wholesale grocery business, the L.M. Stratton Company. Four years later, Leslie Stratton began a dual career in groceries and hardware sales when he joined the wholesale firm Benedict-Warren. He assumed control of the firm and renamed it Stratton-Warren Hardware.

Saunders merged his Saunders-Blackburn wholesale business into Stratton's warehouse and cold storage operations. The Saunders-Stratton Company had one of the largest wholesale grocery businesses in the South with $500,000 capital. The new company purchased the fifteen Piggly Wiggly stores in the Memphis district. Leslie Stratton and his managers assumed daily operations of the stores.

The new arrangement freed Saunders of administrative chores and allowed him to concentrate on selling the Piggly Wiggly system

This is the Piggly Wiggly world headquarters, circa 1923. This building at 461 South Front also served as the wood shop and a warehouse. *Courtesy of Memphis Room, Memphis Public Library and Information Center.*

throughout the country. He began to focus now on selling to investors who could establish multiple stores in larger cities. He had already established Piggly Wiggly stores in forty cities. Five Piggly Wiggly stores opened in Chicago. A writer in *Mother's Magazine* declared, "Thousands in Chicago a few weeks ago...launched a practical declaration of independence against the tyranny of waste, substitution, and high prices." The writer marveled at this odd departure from the traditional grocery operation. "It's as simple as looking out the window or scratching your ear."

Success led to even faster growth for the Piggly Wiggly business. Saunders tried to control his ever-evolving company. In June, he published eight additional brochures describing every detail of his Piggly Wiggly system for his franchisees and employees.

Saunders, the innovator, did not tolerate independent thought from businessmen who bought into his system. Repeatedly, he demanded that no one change anything in a Piggly Wiggly store design. Nor were they

WHATS
and
WHAT NOTS
of
PIGGLY WIGGLY SYSTEM

VOL. 3

In this pamphlet, Saunders supplied a list of merchandise that franchisees were required to stock and a list of thirty-four categories of merchandise that they could not sell. *Courtesy of Special Collections, McWherter Library, University of Memphis.*

By Authority of the Piggly Wiggly Home Office, Memphis, Tenn.
June 1st, 1918

allowed to advertise or promote on their own authority. There was no need for freelance work from the franchisees. The design work and the operating methods had been tested. The mistakes had been made. All the franchisees had to do was follow his rules to make money. Saunders never failed to show investors how they could profit from his ideas. He repeated that the first Piggly Wiggly had substantially higher revenues than his previous store in the same storefront; how he had dramatically lowered his operating costs; how his Piggly Wiggly stores had outperformed a well-run chain of forty-three stores (the Bowers stores).

Piggly Wiggly franchisees sent in their own testimonials to trade magazines. A grocer in Tyler, Texas, who had operated a full-service store for twenty-two years, saw his sales and profits increase when he obtained a Piggly Wiggly franchise. He noticed his competitors maintained a cleaner appearance in their stores in an attempt to offset his Piggly Wiggly advantage.

"A 'Piggly Wiggly,'" an admiring *Commercial Appeal* reporter in 1918 said, "is neither an insect nor a disease; it is a brand new system of retail merchandising and it carries the punch that wins." Visitors came to Memphis—three or four a day, according to the newspaper—just to see the stores. Doubters of the system became believers. People were most curious about that name, Piggly Wiggly. When asked where he found it, Saunders gave various answers, depending on his mood. He could be inscrutable: "Plucked from originality…From out of chaos and in direct contact with an individual's mind."

When asked "Why?" he sometimes snapped, "So people like you can ask me that question." Often he admitted it was the product of calculated thought, that he discarded many names before he discovered the right one. It was easy to recognize and difficult to copy. "Imitators," he wrote, "look at this name with a trembling of their subconscious mind. It says, 'Hands Off!'" He talked about his dissatisfaction with the current retail methods. He offered this comment about his fateful train ride from Terre Haute: "I decided I wouldn't let other people create ideas for me." He insisted that he had never seen a cafeteria or any self-service store before Piggly Wiggly.

Chapter 4

A BUSINESS ROMANCE

Everything he touched turned to gold.

Saunders himself was becoming the subject of journalists' interviews. They noticed that he was a striking individual, a confident, handsome man with prematurely gray hair. The editors of *Judicious Advertising* were impressed with his newspaper ads, which were now being read in many cities, "so very different that people probably thought it crazy, until they got a little used to it." No one knew what to expect when they opened their newspapers to Saunders's advertisements. He fearlessly spouted his opinions and attacked his enemies with little regard for tact or diplomacy. Other businessmen would have thought this tactic suicidal. But Saunders knew his advertisements were being read and that they brought attention to his stores. In fact, his ads actually endeared him to his customers, especially in Memphis. The hometown readers were so familiar with his opinions; they felt they knew him well. And they looked forward to the paper's next edition with its new "Piggly Wiggly installment."

Admirers praised his life story as a parallel to the Horatio Alger novels. One magazine writer described his childhood as "one of the old time business romances that are not met with so often today as they were twenty years ago…It seems the harder time a man has as a boy the bigger success he will make as a man." Stories were published of his youth in Palmyra, homilies of business virtues focusing on personality traits that made him successful: hard work, determination, decisiveness, the will

Many friends called him a genius who had an uncanny ability to concentrate upon each task. He dressed in excellent taste: "There is no atmosphere of flour barrels and cabbages about the Piggly Wiggly man." *Courtesy of the Memphis Room, Memphis Public Library and Information Center.*

to win. Saunders boasted to writers that he was self-confident and determined to succeed when he was only nine years old.

Clarence Saunders had more challenges to meet. He, Leslie Stratton and investors founded the Piggly Wiggly Corporation in August 1918. These investor friends composed the corporation board of directors who, of course, chose Saunders as their president. J.P. Norfleet was appointed vice-president. Chester Walker, Carolyn Saunders's brother, became the secretary and treasurer. Another board member, Robert Jordan, had founded one of the first automobile sales companies in Memphis six years before. On November 4, Joseph Boillin replaced Isaac Tigrett on the board.

The new corporation sold franchise licenses, collected royalties and maintained licensing standards. On September 9, 1918, Saunders signed a contract with the Piggly Wiggly Corporation. In the contract, he sold to the corporation all patents, trademarks and licensing rights to operate the Piggly Wiggly system for $550,000 and fifteen thousand shares of Piggly Wiggly common stock. Specific in his contract agreement were the rights to any future patents of the fixtures or arrangements of self-service stores. The corporation now owned exclusive rights to the name "Piggly Wiggly" and to all trademarked or copyrighted materials. Saunders gave to the corporation the right to use the goodwill of his own name. Although goodwill was a business concept with a somewhat vague definition, it implied that Saunders's new status as a celebrity was of benefit in sales to the corporation.

The turnstile became a symbol, used in advertisements like this one. The Piggly Wiggly Corporation launched the *Turnstile*, a magazine for its franchisees and clients, which was still published as late as 1991. *Courtesy of the Memphis Room, Memphis Public Library and Information Center.*

Saunders no longer wrote all the text of advertisements. John Burch was hired as advertising manager to do that. The spirit of his message and his pugnacious style remained: "Piggly Wiggly is as far ahead of the old-fashioned grocery store as the locomotive is ahead of the stage coach…You make your own selections. No bargaining or haggling. Piggy Wiggly has put the kibosh on hot air, gossip and small talk."

In May 1919, Saunders again revised his publications on Piggly Wiggly. The "National Standard for Piggly Wiggly Store Conduct" covered ninety-seven pages. It described the correct procedure for any possible situation a clerk or store manager would encounter in a Piggly Wiggly store. No detail was too unimportant, even the proper methods for storage of lemons and oranges. Seven pages were devoted to the issue of shoplifting. Everything Saunders had learned about the efficient operations of a grocery store he catalogued in this manual.

The "Piggly Wiggly Store Buildings and Equipment Instructions" guided the new store owner through all the steps of store construction.

PIGGLY WIGGLY SYSTEM
(ORIGINATED BY CLARENCE SAUNDERS)

PIGGLY WIGGLY CONTRACT RE-QUIREMENTS Etc.

MAY 1919

MPHS RM
658.878
S257pc

PIGGLY WIGGLY HOME OFFICE
MEMPHIS, TENN.

Saunders quoted the Harvard Graduate School of Business Research, which pegged the business costs of the average grocer at 17 percent of gross sales. His stores had an average business cost of 5 percent. These statistics were repeated in his advertisements. *Courtesy of the Memphis Room, Memphis Public Library and Information Center.*

In the first paragraph, Saunders demanded all store operators use union labor in the construction and installation work. He was trying to prevent franchisees from using unskilled employers for difficult or dangerous tasks. He also gave union labor a strong endorsement. The *Labor Review Magazine* was grateful: "Mr. Saunders can be depended upon to do the thing that is right."

In "Piggly Wiggly Contract Requirements," Saunders addressed his thoughts to an audience of potential franchisees from all cities above 250,000 in population. Saunders proposed to negotiate his fees, instead of setting a standard rate. The negotiations would include determining the number of stores to be constructed within the city's territory, how quickly they were to be built and how much capital the investor was willing to risk. Saunders also expected the Piggly Wiggly operators in these cities to create their own warehouse and shipping operations. They were to buy, in large volume, merchandise direct from the food

The Piggly Wiggly store location gives clues to Saunders's ideas. The right-hand side of traffic routes, streetcar lines, away from downtown, was the most convenient access for shoppers on the way home from work. *Courtesy of the Library of Congress.*

manufacturer or producer. Such volume purchasing would cut out the wholesaler's profit from the merchandise and help lower costs to Piggly Wiggly stores. Saunders had even proposed the best locations for Piggly Wiggly stores in these cities.

He repeated his message on the value of self-service and his warning to conform to his standards. But he also made an unusual admission: that he was not the first to open a self-service grocery store. He knew of self-service stores in California. (Probably the Alpha-Beta stores owned by Albert Gerrard of Pomona; Gerrard named his stores the "Alpha-Beta" because he had arranged his goods by alphabetical order to help customers find things, according to the *Illustrated World* magazine, January 1916.) There were also self-service stores in other places. Nor did Saunders claim any monopoly on the self-service principle in retail stores. Anyone, he said, could open a self-service grocery store. But they had better not use or copy any of the interior arrangement of Piggly

Wiggly, nor any of the exterior combination of colors. They had better not use any of the property rights now guarded by his patents. He did not copy any self-service store when he designed Piggly Wiggly, and once again, he threatened to prosecute those who copied him. It might take him six years to collect property rights damages, but he would sue. He called imitators "a snoopy oozle-spined creature whose avocation was pussy-footing around the brain workings of an originator."

Could Saunders really hope to collect from those he believed copied his Piggly Wiggly? Saunders had launched a revolution among the retail grocers. They were removing their old fixtures and installing new fixtures to take advantage of self-service. *American Magazine* in 1919 found a typical grocer in Elmira, New York, who, after switching to self-service, sold twice as many groceries in just one day as he expected to sell that week. Several grocers devised their own self-service designs and applied for a patent. Patents for self-service grocery stores were issued to ten inventors by the United States Patent Office between September 1916 and 1921. One of these inventors was Jackson, Mississippi businessman William Bonner McCarty. He opened his stores under the name Jitney Jungle.

Saunders and his lawyers gathered evidence for infringement lawsuits and expected to win. Not content to rely on his lawyers, he made his own study of business law through correspondence courses. He achieved some success against patent and trademark infringement. Some cases were easier than others. On January 16, 1921, St. Louis businessman Charles Tammer was forced to stop using the name Hoggly Woggly for his grocery stores. A month later, the corporation launched two ambitious legal actions. Together these cases were to decide "if the Piggly Wiggly patents on its self-service plan of merchandising were valid or not," stated a wire service report. "More than five hundred stores were using a self-service plan at the time, and they may be liable to Piggly Wiggly, or will be prevented from using the self-service plan in their stores." The amount of compensation Piggly Wiggly wished to collect was $100 million. The corporation retained Charles Evan Hughes, who would become the secretary of state under President Warren Harding, as counsel.

On February 24, 1921, Piggly Wiggly filed suit against John R. Thompson of Chicago. In 1920, Thompson had opened twenty self-service stores, allegedly with a copy of the patented equipment, which misled the public into believing his stores were part of the Piggly

Wiggly chain. It is ironic that Thompson had created the cafeteria, the self-service restaurant, nearly thirty years before in Chicago. He never claimed the principle of self-service for himself, but he adopted it and opened Thompson restaurants in large American cities.

Within the week, on February 28, Piggly Wiggly filed an infringement lawsuit in Denver against the Cash and Carry Stores and other grocery companies. This suit involved 250 "grocerterias," or self-service stores. One of the store owners had lived in Jackson, Tennessee. At some time the corporation filed suit against McCarty and Jitney Jungle. Disposition of the first two legal actions is unknown. Eventually, McCarty won his court case against Piggly Wiggly.

Piggly Wiggly's competitors attacked in other ways. Mr. Bowers' Stores, in Memphis, printed in an ad, "The Grocer Who Serves You…a local institution for Memphis people—by Memphis people—with no idea of spreading it to other cities." Bakery companies in St. Louis refused to sell bread to Piggly Wiggly stores unless they raised the price of bread by a penny. This boycott, encouraged by retail grocery stores, lasted only two days before Piggly Wiggly obtained bread from rival bakeries in Illinois. Such was the fate of those who tried to stop this new idea.

At the end of 1919, Saunders found additional investment capital, an estimated $25 million. Together, he and his capitalists formed Piggly Wiggly Stores, Inc. (the Stores Company). The new company was granted exclusive privilege to create and operate Piggly Wiggly stores. The new company in turn would sell specific territorial rights to investors. Another objective was to combine management of existing stores, where possible, into a single organization. At first the new company acquired 124 of the 300 privately owned franchise stores. Among the stores purchased were the Chicago, St. Louis and Memphis stores.

The Stores Company issued 150,000 shares of Class A common stock and 37,000 shares of privately held Class B preferred stock. The common stock sold at $42 a share on the Chicago Stock Exchange, netting nearly $6 million. The Piggly Wiggly Corporation still collected franchise fees and obtained patents. Not long before, Saunders had sold to the Piggly Wiggly Corporation all rights to patent applications in foreign countries for $210,000 cash and 35,000 shares of common stock. The corporation applied for patents in Canada, England, France, Spain, Cuba and Mexico, with the intention of building stores in those nations someday.

In Memphis, Saunders-Stratton Grocery Co. sold its share in the Memphis Piggly Wiggly stores and then disbanded the partnership. Stratton formed a new wholesale business with one of Saunders's former employers, W.C. Early. The following year, Stratton would resign from the corporation board of directors in order to buy franchises from the Stores Company.

Many of Saunders's employees found Piggly Wiggly's success to be their opportunity. They obtained Piggly Wiggly franchises for themselves. Among them, Milton Magnus left the home office, at vice-president's rank, for Birmingham, Alabama. D.D. Williams began working for Saunders at the United Store and then at the King Piggly Wiggly on Jefferson Avenue. He moved up the organization ranks to a regional manager in the Stores Company. Unhappy there, he asked for a franchise. He was granted San Diego, California, and two portable store units on loan. Within ten years, his Piggly Wiggly San Diego Company would operate twenty-three stores and employ one hundred people. The career of Andrew Williams (no relation) was a short history of the Memphis chain store. Saunders recruited him from the Bowers store, and he helped install the fixtures in the King Piggly Wiggly. In 1919, he moved to Oakland, California, with a borrowed $10,000 and the franchise for Northern California. Andrew Williams prospered. Eventually he owned ninety-six Piggly Wiggly stores and introduced self-service to Hawaii.

Saunders was still giving away flowers when he opened a new Piggly Wiggly, only now on a much grander scale. In Washington, D.C., 100,000 people visited the twenty-six new stores on the grand opening day, May 6, 1920, and received 125,000 carnations. Senator Kenneth McKeller of Tennessee and Senator Underwood of Alabama visited Saunders. The new Piggly Wiggly stores sold $28,000 of groceries that first day. The newspaper ad in the Washington papers showed twenty-six storks, each carrying a baby labeled "Piggly Wiggly." Saunders wrote, "Fluttering baby birds. 'Tis in the Springtime baby birds are born. 'Tis in the Springtime that new flowers burst forth with new born life."

Piggly Wiggly Stores, Inc., owned and operated 393 stores by the end of its first year. Saunders's idea was now a national enterprise. The Stores Company organized its warehouse and administrative system at considerable expense. Also, the decline in food prices during the postwar economic slump in the fall of 1920 matched a disastrous drop in the stock value, from forty dollars a share to ten. It climbed quickly back to eighteen dollars. Even during this downturn, store earnings increased every quarter. The net profit for Piggly Wiggly Stores, Inc., in 1921 was $208,062. Gross sales were $30,210,420. Company officials were satisfied with any profit in 1921, a year when many companies showed a loss or declared bankruptcy.

Analysts predicted that Piggly Wiggly Stores, Inc., stock prices would move up to the $35 to $40 range when the company's earnings increased. They expected administrative costs to vary little after the first year. Then new store openings would increase the sales of the company and provide a lower average operating cost for the entire chain. Profits of the company would increase with each new store. A typical Piggly Wiggly store sold as much as $3,000 to $5,000 of goods a week. Experts were convinced that self-service was the most profitable retail arrangement and the business trend of the future. Roger Babson, the business statistician and columnist, compared store earnings of Piggly Wiggly with the Atlantic and Pacific Tea Company, the largest chain grocery store company with over four thousand stores. The A&P had eliminated charge accounts and delivery service in 1912, but the company still employed clerks to wait on shoppers. Annual sales per store of the A&P in 1920 were $50,000, less than half of the Piggly Wiggly sales number of $120,000. Babson predicted the great A&P chain would have to follow Piggly Wiggly's example and switch to self-service.

Clarence Saunders turned forty on August 9, 1921. In September 1921, at the fifth anniversary of Piggly Wiggly, Saunders boasted of his achievements. His companies owned or leased 615 stores in two hundred cities in forty states. Their combined sales were now $60 million. Piggly Wiggly was the largest user of newspaper advertising space in the country—ten thousand inches of space per week, double the amount of any other newspaper advertiser. Piggly Wiggly was the third-largest chain of grocery stores in the nation. Given its then current rate of growth, it seemed destined to be the largest retail grocery business. Saunders expected nothing less than the top for Piggly Wiggly. Only a fraction of the estimated 360,000 grocery stores in the nation used self-service, a Piggly Wiggly Corporation executive bragged to *Financial World* magazine. The estimated target was to build 8,000 Piggly Wiggly stores.

Saunders began his lifelong habit of buying expensive possessions, like this four-door convertible. *Courtesy of the Memphis Room, Memphis Public Library and Information Center.*

Saunders achieved a level of celebrity and wealth that most people only dream of. Games of intricate strategy and skill satisfied him most of all. Bridge challenged his analytical mind. He played to win, mastering the game well enough to beat a touring expert of the game. The game of golf was his most celebrated passion. Saunders played his golf now at the Memphis Country Club. The club was exclusive and patrician, where bloodlines counted as much as bank accounts. Saunders played the game in his unique way, splurging on bets and caddie tips. The crowd of eager golfers and caddies surrounding him reportedly did not fit the decorum club directors wished to project. He was at best a mediocre player. His awkward stroke, according to one member of the family, "resembled Donald Duck when teeing off." Then he would stride down the course as rapidly as possible to hit his next shot. But he was not one to be made a fool of. A hustling golf professional, observing his skill and spending

Saunders bought the Johnson estate at Lamar and Central, the probable location of this photo. He enjoyed sportsman's hobbies and vigorous exercise. The physical activity kept him in excellent shape. *Courtesy of the Memphis Room, Memphis Public Library and Information Center.*

habits, agreed to play Saunders for a little money. The pro deliberately lost a hole, hoping Saunders would "play the sucker" and increase the size of his bets. Saunders saw the hustle. He stopped playing and turned to him. "Listen! I'm paying you and we are betting on each hole. If I win a hole fine, but you do your best. If I don't win, so what! Don't try that again! Don't make a chump out of me!"

He also forged a new role: civic leader. In October 1920, he gave $27,500 to fund a campus in Memphis for a school in Clarksville, Southwestern Presbyterian College. In 1924, the school opened its new campus. It is now called Rhodes College.

The demands on his time, and the pleasures of wealth, did not distract Saunders from his goals. On November 18, 1921, he fulfilled another of his merchandising dreams: opening a self-service variety store. Some people thought Saunders had made an unwise decision. He had leased the old cafe of the Peabody Hotel at Main and Monroe for his store.

The lease with the Memphis Hotel Company, owner of the Peabody Hotel, was one of the most expensive rentals in the city. Saunders faced tough competition. Nearby on Main Street were several variety stores, including one of the oldest chain stores, S.H. Kresge. He was not intimidated by tradition or competition. He predicted, in the grand opening advertisement, that he would soon have two thousand Piggly Wiggly Variety Stores: "In the Southland, in the city of Memphis on the banks of the Mississippi, where romance clings to every hour of days gone by, where the mighty pulse of the throbbing TODAY makes new things out of old and new things where was nothing before."

He called his seven low prices the "Seven Newest Wonders of the World, 4 cents, 9 cents, 13 cents, 19 cents, 23 cents, 29 cents, 39 cents." He marked all his items in a similar fashion to the five and dime stores. Saunders had demonstrated that self-service was practical in the variety merchandise or five and dime stores, even though not all items a variety store handled were suitable for self-service. Shoppers still needed the services of sales clerks for more luxurious goods and for items offering various styles and sizes. Saunders employed clerks to sell jewelry, candy, music, ribbons and lace. Other chain store companies in the drug and sundry business remodeled their stores for self-service. Like Saunders, they discovered that self-service was generally successful for products that were inexpensive and required little salesmanship from clerks.

Thousands of people crowded into the Variety Store during the grand opening. Doubters watched the sales and once again realized that he was right. Saunders and thirty of his Stores Company employees celebrated with a banquet dinner at the Hotel Chisca. It was curious that a man who garnered so much attention was shy at times. While Saunders watched the grand opening festivities, a silhouette artist for the *Memphis News-Scimitar* sketched his portrait. Saunders blushed "like a school girl" when the artist presented him with it.

In February 1922, Clarence Saunders reached another milestone in business. The New York Stock Exchange listed Piggly Wiggly Stores Inc. Class A common stock. In April 1922, the company sold fifty thousand new shares of common stock on the markets at $43 a share, earning over $2 million.

As the analysts predicted, the earnings for Piggly Wiggly increased dramatically in 1922. Piggly Wiggly had managed the economic depression well. Having stores in every region of the country became quite an advantage, for an economic depression often has an uneven effect upon the regions. Stores in one area prospered enough to offset the stores in a more depressed region. The net profit of the Stores Company in 1922 was $653,058, earning stockholders $3.26 per share on the 200,000 shares. The Stores Company doubled the quarterly dividend for the common stock to $2.

Saunders was ready to indulge in his greatest reward. Early in the spring of 1922, he purchased a 160-acre tract of land east of the city for over $160,000. In May, he unveiled plans for his new country estate. The house would face the Memphis Country Club, located just south of his property on Central Avenue. North of the house he designed an eighteen-hole golf course. A 5-acre lake was to grace the back nine. On the estate grounds were to be tennis and handball courts, riding trails, a trap shoot area, formal gardens, a table garden and a pasture for his farm animals and saddle horses. Saunders planned a self-sufficient estate. Separate buildings would house a pumping station and generator for utilities, a refrigeration plant and cold storage room, a laundry and garage.

The house was roughly U shaped with two wings and was of immense proportions, 200 feet long across the front and 150 feet on each wing. Its design was described as "rambling Spanish style or Romanesque American." Protruding bays, multiple-paned windows and a green tile roof of French mansard style were to be its distinctive characteristics. The main entrance was to be magnificent, with circular steps leading to a broad porch supported by arched columns, all made of carved limestone. The hardwood structure was covered with a limestone and pink Georgia marble veneer. In one wing, Saunders planned a grand ballroom and a separate room for a motion picture projector and screen. Underneath he wanted a billiards room and bowling alley. In the opposite wing, he planned an indoor swimming pool in the basement.

Hubert McGee, the architect, drew the blueprint specifications for Saunders's ideas. But Saunders acted as his own designer and construction supervisor. Nothing was too small to escape his attention. One day, Saunders noticed workmen idle and an expected shipment of stone not present. When he inquired why, he was told no one could find trucks to deliver the stones. Saunders exploded. Rent mules to haul stones, he ordered. Soon a mule train was observed making its way through the city streets to the Saunders estate.

Saunders had announced that the estate would be named "Cla-Le-Clare" after his three children. Clay was now twelve years old, Lee was fifteen and away at school and Amy Clare was nine. But after watching the stonemasons install the pink marble over the building frame, Memphians dubbed the house its enduring name, the Pink Palace.

Next, Saunders turned his creative promotional talents to help Austin Peay, a prominent tobacco planter and lawyer from Clarksville. Peay at the turn of the century had married Sally Hurst, the daughter of John Hurst, one of Saunders's employers at Boillin-Hurst. Four years earlier, Peay had asked Saunders to help in his campaign for governor. Saunders organized a parade in the city streets with all the excitement of a Piggly Wiggly show. "Folks like noise," he later said. "This is going to be a real election with all the trimmings." Peay lost then and, in 1922, was ready to try again.

That year also marked the rise of a new generation of politicians into leadership in Tennessee. Austin Peay, just forty-six, ran against Benton McMillin in the Democratic primary for governor. McMillin had earlier served two terms as governor and was now seventy-seven years old. In his advertisement, Saunders gently handled the issue of age. He honored McMillin as the noble war horse who had won many a battle for the cause. But now was the time for a younger steed to take on the fight. Peay won the primary.

Peay's opponent in the November election was the Republican governor Alfred Taylor, seeking reelection after his 1920 victory. (Tennessee governors served two-year terms then.) In 1886, Governor Alfred Taylor ran against his brother Robert Taylor, a Democrat, for the governor of Tennessee. Older Tennesseans fondly remembered when "Uncle Alf" and "Uncle Bob" shared the same speakers' platform on the campaign trail, swapping yarns about hunting dogs between rounds of fiddle playing. Governor Taylor, in 1922, still played his fiddle and spoke of his favorite dog, "Old Limber." In contrast, Peay lectured quietly to the voters on the need for better roads, tax reform and greater efficiency in state government.

Saunders seized upon the disparities between the two men. In his advertisement, "Foxes Red and Gray," he again paid tribute to the older man. Then he pleaded for voters to accept a more modern candidate: "We just must love him…it makes us happy all over to follow his 'Old Limber' stories…yet there are whispers within us that tells us there is some work to be done…there is some business at hand."

Austin Peay faced a difficult challenge in this race. Edward Hull Crump worked to dominate local elections through his office of county trustee and as head of the Democratic Party organization. His opposition labeled him the "boss" of Memphis and Shelby County government. Few people in Memphis had the courage to openly defy Mr. Crump. Senator Kenneth McKellar and Peay came to Memphis on October 29, a week before the election. The senator had hoped to arrange a meeting with the candidate and Edward Crump that would lead to a united effort among Democratic Party leaders. Crump seemed open to the visit with the understanding that Peay would make certain promises to him. Peay visited Saunders after arriving at Memphis. From Saunders's home, Peay said that he did not want Crump's endorsement. Miffed, Crump made an unusual decision—he endorsed the Republican governor.

Peay and Saunders blasted Crump in speeches and advertisements. "Austin Peay," Saunders wrote, "had rather remain a real man and not be the next governor of Tennessee than be the 'tool,' or the whining puppet of the Political Boss." Peay made one last campaign stop in Memphis on election eve. He was escorted to the Pantages Theater by a torch light parade and brass bands. Faithful Democrats cheered him and Saunders, seated together on the platform dais. One contemporary said Saunders's exuberant style was not to Austin Peay's tastes. The candidate, though, was a shrewd man. He saw that night, as he had in 1918, hundreds of potential voters enthusiastic for him in Memphis, a town ruled by an adversary. At the Pantages Theater, Austin Peay expressed his deep gratitude for the service his campaign manager and friend had given.

Austin Peay won the election for governor on November 8 by thirty thousand votes. He carried Memphis and Shelby County by a majority of only seven hundred votes. The Crump machine gave thousands of votes—fraudulent votes, claimed the *Commercial Appeal*—to Governor Taylor. That Peay had a majority at all was due to Saunders. His work earned praise from the *Christian Science Monitor*: "The triumph of the new age advertising over bossism and the minstrel show campaigns."

Clarence Saunders had helped elect his friend governor. He seemed to be "the mythical king from whose hand everything he touched turned to gold." Saunders was ready, then, to launch a new issue of fifty thousand shares of common stock.

Chapter 5
THE CORNER

Shall the speculator rule?

In hindsight, he had expanded his business too quickly. He sold franchises to some individuals who were not able to operate the stores. On the same day he announced his new stock issue, November 18, 1922, Elliot Business Builders, the Piggly Wiggly licensee in New York, and three of its subsidiary companies filed bankruptcy. The timing of these two events could not have been less fortunate.

Professional stock traders seized the opportunity presented by the licensee bankruptcy to sell Piggly Wiggly stock short. The short sell— or the bear raid, as it is sometimes called—involved selling stock the brokers did not own by borrowing the shares from the "floating pool" of stock available to all brokers. The success of this speculation game was dependent upon the value of the stock dropping in the future. The traders were obligated to pay for the borrowed shares within a specific period of time. If all went well, they bought the shares back at a cheaper price than they had originally sold them for and returned the stock to the "floating pool." In this manner, they reaped a profit from the sale at the earlier higher value less the amount they paid to repurchase the shares. It was a risky way to make money. If the stock had actually increased in price, the speculator paid the difference out of his pocket.

Saunders was furious at these cynical traders who exploited the licensee problem to knock down the value of Piggly Wiggly stock. With investors

Traders who sold "short" picked businesses new to the markets, perhaps with less stable financial clout. News of a financial problem at a Piggly Wiggly licensee made this stock ideal for a bear raid. This is a certificate from that licensee. *Courtesy of the Memphis Pink Palace Museum.*

fleeing the company, they had spoiled his plans to issue new shares. He vowed to break their bear raid and beat them at their own game. He immediately bought every existing share of Piggly Wiggly offered for sale—thirty-three thousand the first day—in order to drive the value of the stock above the price at which the short seller had borrowed. This strategy would force them to repay their commitments at a loss.

Stock market battles have their costs. He bought the shares on "margin," which requires a partial payment down, with the balance due to the stockbroker on a certain date. "Wall Street soaks up money like a sponge," one of his peers recalled. Saunders "poured money into marginal investment like water." He had depleted the Piggly Wiggly Corporation treasury by November 21, 1922, and committed $800,000 of his fortune.

Saunders sought the advice of an expert market operator, Jesse Livermore, the "Boy Plunger of Wall Street." Livermore had earned that nickname from his uncanny ability to predict market trends and the nerve to risk millions on a hunch. Livermore's reputation for stock price forecasting was so great that President Harding consulted with him in 1922 about creating prosperity during his administration.

Livermore presented his plan to Saunders, a game of stealth with the short sellers. Because he did not actually trade on the Exchange floor, Livermore relied on Frank Bliss, the "Silver Fox of Wall Street." Bliss cleverly disguised his trade actions so that market observers could not tell if he was short or long on a stock, until he completed his goal. Bliss and his proxy brokers bought Piggly Wiggly shares on the market; at the same time, he offered shares on loan to the short sellers as if he was cooperating with them. Gradually, he raised the interest payments on the borrowed stock until they found there was no profit in their speculation. To further mask their intentions, Saunders continued to say that Piggly Wiggly would issue the new shares of stock. The Stores Company stock on November 29 closed at $46.50 on the Chicago Exchange. Elated, Saunders hungered for more.

The corner was the ultimate tactic against the short sale. The trader seeking a corner bought every share of stock available until the floating market pool of stock vanished. Holding all the stock, he now called for delivery from the short sellers of the borrowed shares. The trapped short sellers had, by Exchange law, one day to pay their commitments. They had two equally miserable options: either buy the required shares from the holder at an arbitrary price he demanded and then return the shares back to the holder or make a cash settlement to the holder.

A half century before, stock corners were common, the *New York Times* reported, when Cornelius Vanderbilt trapped many a speculator who sold his railroad stocks short. In those days, when a speculator was caught short, "he grinned and paid" or risked prison for not meeting his obligations. Corners often stirred panic among the speculators caught short and sometimes engineered an entire collapse of the market. This was the case in the Great Northern Pacific corner of 1901. Investors, some innocent of the manipulations involved, lost millions of dollars. The New York Stock Exchange discouraged speculators from playing the "game of corner," and wise stock market operators "avoided corners as they did the plague."

More recently, a stock trader had ruined his fortunes after gaining a corner. Allan Ryan in March 1920 tried to extort from the short sellers of the

Stutz Automotive $700 a share and asked that the stock be taken off active trading. The Exchange did so and further stripped Ryan of his seat on the Exchange, then worth more than $50,000. It suspended the rules concerning delivery to protect the short sellers from Ryan's demands. Ryan, in financing the corner, overextended himself and was forced into bankruptcy.

Saunders either did not read the *Times* or ignored Wall Street history. He let his most loyal friends in the corporation in on his plans. Fletcher Scott, Walter Smith and Chester Walker pledged to him their shares of stock. In return, they received a down payment in cash. Soon, he told them, he planned to squeeze from the Wall Streeters millions of dollars on the stock. The value of the stock would be worth whatever price he fixed. Then he would repay his friends their part of the profit. Scott expected to make $105,000 on his 1,500 shares of stock.

Saunders organized a pool of Memphis investors who spent $1 million on November 30. He offered to these investors as collateral the Piggly Wiggly common stock bought on margin. The pool members advanced money at $30 a share. In the same manner, he procured $480,000 from friends in Nashville. Saunders also obtained $960,000 from forty businessmen in St. Louis through his Piggly Wiggly connections. His high-stakes gamble attracted attention in Chicago: "He has succeeded in stirring up a great deal of interest in his pet stock along LaSalle Street. Neither Chick Evans or Walter Hagan [the professional golfers] has ever enjoyed a larger gallery than is following Piggly Wiggly gyrations these days on the Chicago Exchange."

The Chicago traders gave Saunders a warning. He was playing in a game he did not understand. They had enough money to pay all the obligations he was now demanding through Livermore and Bliss. So let him have his corner. Soon they would break it. The New York Stock Exchange also took notice of Saunders. The Board of Governors of the Exchange summoned him to explain why he had abandoned plans to launch a new issue of Piggly Wiggly stock. Reportedly, he traveled to New York with over $1 million stuffed into suitcases.

The Chicago traders were correct. Saunders had pushed himself into a difficult position. Brokers began to demand full payment in cash for the stock he purchased on margin; his potential debt was enormous. He kept all but a few Piggly Wiggly Corporation directors unaware of the debt he had created for himself and for the corporation. At a directors' meeting on December 29, Saunders presented a glowing picture of the corporation's future and even approved of a double dividend for stockholders. He then called his old friend Robert Jordan aside and said he needed $50,000 that day or the speculation would fail. Only then did he and James McRee discover the extent to which Saunders had depleted the treasury.

Saunders searched for more money. Again relying on his grocery connections, he organized a pool of New Orleans investors. A.W. Beardon, president of the Piggly Wiggly franchise company in that city and a bank director, was an investor. Another pool member was Lynn Dinkins, president of the Interstate Trust and Banking Company. Saunders offered them the same deal as the earlier pools: Stores Company stock bought on margin at thirty dollars a share. Dinkins, in turn, helped Saunders obtain loans from two New York banks.

After the board meeting of January 30, 1923, Saunders, with some of the board members, called upon Rogers Caldwell, who had invested in the Nashville pool. Caldwell directed Caldwell and Company, an interlocking network of banks, insurance and finance companies in Nashville. His corporate interests extended through several states. He had considerable influence in Tennessee government. His banks held some of the deposits for the state treasury. Saunders negotiated from the financier a $1 million loan in the name of the Piggly Wiggly Corporation. Caldwell drove a hard bargain. He demanded a 10 percent commission for his services in arranging the loan through his companies and other investors. Together, Caldwell and his investors received as collateral fifty thousand shares of the corporation's Class B preferred stock. Caldwell intended to have a major role in Piggly Wiggly affairs.

The value of the stock had risen from fifty dollars at the first of the year to near sixty dollars in February. The shorts were now under pressure from Saunders. Since fewer shares were available in the actual market supply—Saunders had cornered so much—the shorts were in effect bidding up the price of the shares just to repay their commitments.

Saunders paid off margin debts with some of the invested money, thereby gaining possession of thousands of shares. Still short of cash, Saunders did not want to hold on to all of the shares, yet he had no desire to place them back on the markets within the grasp of the speculators. With his friend, stockbroker Bernard Bogy, he devised a new company.

Their Piggly Wiggly Investment Company sold Piggly Wiggly Stores, Inc., shares to people outside of the financial districts. They offered the stock at fifty-five dollars, payable on the installment plan, twenty-five dollars down and three ten-dollar installments. That price was below the quotations on the Exchanges. Saunders placed newspaper advertisements throughout the West and the South for the Piggly Wiggly Investment Company. In the ads, he assumed the role of the white knight fighting the evil speculators: "Shall the gambler rule? On a high horse he rides. Bluff is his coat of mail and thus shielded is a yellow heart. His helmet is deceit and the hoofbeats of his horse thunder destruction…Shall good business flee? Shall it tremble with fear? Shall it be the loot of the speculator?"

Saunders had an easy sell. Within a month, people bought fifty-seven thousand shares, sending $1,425,000 to the Piggly Wiggly Investment Company. Saunders used that money to pay off margin investment.

The stock value rose in February and March to past seventy dollars. Rumors spread in the markets of a squeeze, that Saunders held enough shares now to close the pool of stock available for borrowing. The New York Stock Exchange's business conduct committee began an inquiry on his stock trade. They asked brokers to identify who had purchased, sold or loaned shares of the stock since the beginning of the short sell campaign. They summoned Saunders to New York for a meeting on March 12. The committee asked him to stop selling stock in his ads for less than the market quotation and to continue maintaining a supply of stock for the shorts. He agreed to do both.

Livermore was concerned about his client. He knew that several brokers who had sold Piggly Wiggly short were complaining to the Exchange about Saunders. He also knew Wall Street history. It was urgent, he said to Saunders, that they meet in New York the same day he was to appear at the Exchange's inquiry. Saunders thought the cool stock operator had lost his nerve during their meeting: "He gave me the impression that he was a little afraid of my financial condition and that he did not care to be involved in any market crash." Livermore warned Saunders that he could no longer ask for obligations due in Piggly Wiggly stock. With their position so dangerous, he urged Saunders to give the shorts a break.

Saunders was in no mood to compromise with Wall Street speculators. He told Livermore to place orders for more stock. Livermore replied with an emphatic "No!" Saunders fired him. "When I left Mr. Livermore,"

Saunders later said, "I told him that I would handle entirely all buying orders in the future." After rumors that the Exchange would suspend trading in Piggly Wiggly shares, the stock dropped from $80.00 to $65.25.

Clarence Saunders spent approximately $12 million in the speculation, risking everything he owned with an abiding faith that he would win. The Exchange could not stop him from demanding delivery of shares the short sellers did not possess, and by Exchange law the short sellers had to honor their commitments to him within one day.

Saunders already planned to spend his new wealth in Memphis. He refused to surrender the five-year lease to his Piggly Wiggly Variety Store. His decision frustrated the Memphis Hotel Company, owners of the Peabody Hotel, and Robert Snowden, president of the National Bank of Commerce and Trust. Together they had arranged to turn over the old hotel property to Lowensteins Department Store, after which they would construct a new Peabody Hotel at Second and Union. Instead, Saunders announced plans to build his own hotel at Main and Monroe, the site of the Peabody Hotel.

On Tuesday, March 20, Clarence Saunders made his final battle charge. He called for delivery of his Piggly Wiggly stock on the Exchanges. The traders who sold short were caught by Saunders. They desperately bid for shares, advancing the price from $1 to $6 during sales. Fully one-third of the brokers on the floor of the New York Stock Exchange crowded about the Piggly Wiggly post. They found themselves unable to put their hands on enough stock; one broker lost $60,000 that day. In one hour, the stock climbed to a peak of $124 a share, a net gain of 52 points above the opening value of $72. The brokerage houses refused to accept orders unless the seller could produce the actual stock certificates for delivery, rare in stock trade and a notice that the corner had been realized.

The corner produced an unexpected windfall to a retired grocer from Providence, Rhode Island. He had bought one thousand shares of Piggly Wiggly the previous fall at $38 outright and planned to hold on to them. Upon hearing the call for delivery, he traveled to New York with his certificates. He sold shares at prices from $96 to $124 a share and profited close to $80,000. Livermore and Bliss sold their shares that morning before Saunders launched the corner and moved to put as much distance between themselves and the corner as possible. "I never conducted any transactions in this stock for my own account," Livermore said to the press.

The business conduct committee of the New York Stock Exchange (the Chicago Exchange acted in concert with the NYSE in this case) held an emergency meeting. They moved to calm the short sellers by letting it be known that the board of governors would suspend trade in Piggly Wiggly after the close of business. The tactic worked. Selling orders flooded the market. The stock dropped, to the relief of the shorts, forty-two points to eighty-two dollars, where it closed. None of the other traded stocks was affected by the Piggly Wiggly corner. The feared market panic did not occur.

A financial writer of the *New York Times* expressed his displeasure with Saunders:

> *Yesterday's performance of the stock of a chain-store supply enterprise with the extremely dignified title "Piggly Wiggly"…was in a way a humiliation to the Stock Exchange because of the relative unimportance of the enterprise concerned. No doubt we shall hear, as we did after the Stutz performance, appeals to the public of the "high-handed methods" of the Stock Exchange Governing Committee. There are times, however, when prompt and thorough-going action of this sort is the only safeguard which the market and the public can have against the reckless misuse of the opportunities by manipulators and thimble-riggers.*

The next day, March 21, the board of governors suspended trade in Piggly Wiggly Stores, Inc., stock from the Exchange until further notice. They demanded the perpetrator of the corner explain his actions. Ernest Bradford, representing Saunders in New York, did not protest the suspension.

Saunders talked to newsmen at home that day. He was proud of himself and let them know what he thought of his corner: "A razor to my throat, figuratively speaking, is why I suddenly and without warning kicked the pegs from under Wall Street…No company of which I am president will ever be permitted to be traded on the Exchange."

He demanded the shorts settle their accounts in full with him by three o'clock that afternoon, with either the stock certificates or $150 cash. After his deadline, he would charge $250 per share. He claimed he controlled 198,872 of the 200,000 shares of the stock. The short sellers owed him 25,000 of those shares. He declined to guess how much money he had made from the corner, but estimates of a $10 million profit were talked about.

Memphians shared in his triumph. The *Commercial Appeal* crowed, "New York speculators...had been made to pay through the nose." A businessman during a chamber of commerce luncheon was quoted: "Memphis is perhaps better known and advertised by the fact that it is the home of Piggly Wiggly than by any other thing...Instead of having only one such man... [I] wish Memphis had 25 like him. More power to him."

Clarence Saunders had a good portion of the country pulling for him. Harper Leach reminisced in his newspaper column of youth in a simpler, more pastoral age, a boyhood he and Saunders had shared. He was a Chicago newspaper columnist who had grown up in Clarksville and once edited a Memphis newspaper in 1908: "Few of us lack a bit of the Old Homestead slant of life that makes us grin when the 'yap' puts it all over on the city 'slicker.' That's why the Saunders episode will appeal to the great majority." His victory on Wall Street and impudent treatment of the Exchange members touched upon shared fears of distant, cold financiers and greedy speculators. In the following newspaper editorials, Saunders was a hero:

> *There is a bunch a smart gentry away out on a wabbling limb, with Clarence Saunders (of Memphis Tenn-o-see) sawing away at said limb. It is a pathetic picture.*

> *Clarence Saunders, a golden fleeced lamb from Tennessee, recently wandered into Wall Street...and sheared its Jasons.*

> *Piggly Wiggly—'tis a name to conjure with, apparently a stroke of genius itself. To think of a nursery rhyme innocent like Piggly Wiggly straying into Wall Street, turning out to be a wolf and gobbling up the old habitués of the jungle! The joke is certainly not on Saunders.*

At the moment he received the most applause on the national stage, Saunders's victory over Wall Street collapsed. The joke, unfortunately, was on Clarence Saunders. On March 21, Bradford appeared before the Law Committee of the Exchange and informed them that $150 was the minimum price Mr. Saunders would accept for the shares. "It was a reasonable figure in view of the fact Mr. Saunders had them in a trap." Asked why Saunders did not keep his assurance on March 12 that he would keep a supply of stock available for brokers to borrow so they could keep their commitments, Bradford calmly replied, "The circumstances had changed." He then pleaded with the Law Committee not to suspend the stock indefinitely, as this would be unfair to Saunders. He asked that a time be fixed for delivery and the suspension of trading lifted by March 26.

Instead, the board of governors (of both the New York and Chicago Exchanges), noting his sarcastic remarks, punished Clarence Saunders. On Thursday, March 22, they ordered the stock of the Piggly Wiggly Stores, Inc., permanently stricken from trade. They extended the time of delivery from one day to five working days. Monday, March 26, was the new deadline for the shorts to cover their commitments in Stores Company stock. The editors of the *New York Times* later chuckled:

> *A nation at least 66⅔ "sucker" had its moment of triumph when it read that a sucker had trimmed the interests and had his foot on Wall Street's neck while vicious manipulators gasped their lives away…Saunders waved his sword and thumped his shield and went back to Memphis to tell the folks about it, and wicked Wall Street was up at the count of nine, with its winds fresh, ready for another round.*

Few of the shorts brought the stipulated price of $150 to Bradford for settlement. Other traders, sensing their adversary's weakened position, came to him and bluntly said they would not pay. The five days to fulfill the short sellers' obligations allowed these men precious time to find holders of the stock. They had purchased some shares "over the counter," on the curb Exchanges. More importantly, they enticed many of the investors who had bought stock at Saunders's request and exploited another flaw in Saunders's plan. While Saunders claimed he "controlled" over 198,000 shares of Piggly Wiggly, he did not own all those shares and, really, could not prevent a sale.

Some shareholders couldn't resist taking advantage of the high prices— between $100 and $145 for shares—offered by the brokers. Saunders bitterly watched men he had counted on sell their blocks of stock for big profits. He trusted them and they, some of them prominent members of the community, had double-crossed him.

All his life Saunders was convinced he was cheated, a belief his family and friends share today. But he was not the only one who lost money in Piggly Wiggly. One Memphian recalled that his father and others among Saunders's allies lost money because they held the stock too long.

His bankers were pressing him now to end the affair and settle at any price. On Friday, March 23, he dropped his settlement price to $100 per share. Trying to maintain appearances, he and Bradford contended that the move was motivated by generosity and a desire to get back to the business of running grocery stores. The curb market price for Piggly Wiggly stock dropped below $100. The shorts found enough shares to deliver certificates to Saunders rather than the cash settlement. One broker said that the Twentieth Century Limited arrived from Chicago with a "fair sized bundle of Piggly Wiggly stock certificates." Virtually all the short sellers delivered an estimated seven to ten thousand shares that day to Bradford.

Saunders remained defiant as his financial position grew worse, and he claimed he wouldn't take the stock offered as settlement for even $1,000 a share. Their stock was purchased after Wednesday, which was illegal, he said, since trade in Piggly Wiggly was suspended on that day. The New York Stock Exchange had violated another of its rules when it allowed its members to cover their commitments in five days instead of the prescribed one day. The stock market speculators dodged a fair settlement with him with the assistance of the Exchange. He was strident: "We have a law against common gambling and lottery chances in this country and certainly we need a law that will penalize the higher form of gambling and lottery chances as it is practiced through the New York Stock Exchange."

Calling it "the worst menace in its power to ruin all who dare oppose it…a law unto itself," he announced that he would soon file suit against the Exchange. He retained the law firm of Ewing, Allen and Voorhees to prepare his legal actions. A related lawsuit was filed in November 1923. Walter Smith and Frank Milton, both investors of Piggly Wiggly, filed suit against the New York Stock Exchange and three member firms. Saunders was not formally a party in the suit, although Ewing, Allen and Voorhees represented Smith and Milton. Their action was considered a test case. Smith and Milton estimated they lost $100,000 on the stock.

Later, Exchange president Seymor Cromwell contended in court that Saunders's own corner activities were illegal on the Exchange and that

Saunders had violated previous agreements with the Exchange. Drastic measures, he argued, were necessary to stop him, and the Exchange was within its rights to suspend its own rules in such an emergency. Cromwell successfully defended the suit.

Business historians differ on whether the Exchange treated Saunders with fairness or not. Many did see the Piggly Wiggly corner as one of the more spectacular trading episodes in the Roaring Twenties. Grocery men had their own theories about the Piggly Wiggly corner. "The shoemaker sticks to his shoes, the grocery man sticks to his onions," they liked to say. To them, Saunders had grown too big for his own good and acted like he knew something about everything. He should have never bothered with Wall Street, should have never left his grocery stores.

Chapter 6
SAVE PIGGLY WIGGLY
FOR MEMPHIS

Clarence Saunders is not broke till Memphis is broke.

O n March 26, Saunders reluctantly accepted the delivery of Piggly
Wiggly stock from the short sellers. He had nothing to show for his
efforts in the stock market but nearly 200,000 certificates and a $3 million
debt. His pool of investors gave up any hope of making a profit from
Wall Street. They wanted their money refunded soon and quietly, without
depending on his proposed lawsuit. "Trust me, I will get you out," he promptly
replied. On Wednesday, March 28, he launched another sale of stock on
the installment plan through the Piggly Wiggly Investment Company. "It
would be a disgrace to have my stocks handled anywhere about Wall Street,"
he declared. "I will sell directly to the people." If they bought the stock,
he would pay his debts and end this messy affair. Page ads were printed in
many newspapers offering the stock at $55 a share. The terms were easy:
$10 down and a $5 payment per month. He expected to sell 100,000 shares.

But sales lagged. He then started a mail-order campaign. The
Investment Company sent out brochures that predicted Piggly Wiggly
sales of $100 million for 1923. Still the stock did not sell. Saunders fumed.
The Wall Streeters, through their banking connections, spread the word
around the country not to buy the stock, that it wasn't worth $55. Even
bankers in Memphis frowned upon the campaign.

Saunders tried one more campaign to sell the stock. With the help of
friends, he would sell to Memphians who trusted him, not Wall Street

or the bankers. In his ad, on May 2, he proposed that every household buy at least one share of Piggly Wiggly Stores, Inc., stock. He called upon their civic pride and their indignation over his unfair treatment by the Exchange.

"Wall Street is right," he began, "…when it says that unless I sell the Piggly Wiggly stock I will go broke." He made it clear that neither he nor his friends, who invested millions in the stock, earned a nickel from the transactions. His friends, he pointed out, did not complain and remained loyal to him. He could have made a fortune short selling the stock last fall, he carefully explained, but he chose not to take advantage of his stockholders. That some stockholders took advantage of his predicament, he insisted, did not embitter him. He supposed they thought themselves brilliant by selling shares to the Wall Street brokers.

He then closed: "If I did not owe for money borrowed on this stock, which loans I wish to pay, I would not sell a single share." He pleaded for volunteers to help him sell the stock to others "because it is a good investment first, and the right thing to do for the good of Memphis and for the public generally."

Memphians' response was immediate and genuine. More than 350 friends came to a banquet in his honor at the Hotel Gayoso the next evening. A reporter from the *Commercial Appeal* was excited by the event: "It was the most remarkable demonstration of civic loyalty that Memphis has witnessed since the stirring days of the Civil War." The newspaper's editor, C.P.J. Mooney, shared his enthusiasm: "Memphis spoke with the voice of a giant for Clarence Saunders and his enterprise. Piggly Wiggly…is worth the while of Memphis and this large cross section of the citizenry realized last night."

Many spoke of their affection for Saunders at the banquet. The Reverend C.C. Grimes, pastor of his church, St. John's Methodist, said, "The Piggly Wiggly idea was born of genuine religious motive…the system puts food on the table of those who are compelled to count their pennies. In this respect they are rendering a great service to humanity." Bernard Cohn, editor of the *News Scimitar*, concurred: "Wall Street may strip him of his money and personal effects, but they can never strip him of his indomitable courage that cannot be measured in dollars and cents." Guston Fitzhugh expressed similar thoughts: "The spirit of this meeting is evidence Memphis has a heart and soul." Robert R. Ellis, former president of the chamber of commerce, followed him: "The eyes of the country are on Memphis. People all over the country talk about Saunders and wish him well."

Clarence and Carolyn Saunders were greeted with spontaneous applause as they entered the banquet room. At the podium, he said, "What happens to me is of little consequence, but the prosperity and good will of Memphis is of great moment." Steve Butler, chairing the banquet affair, pledged that all three thousand members of the chamber would sell fifty thousand shares of Piggly Wiggly stock. At the $55 asking price, they hoped to bring in $2,500,000 for Saunders. Butler named a committee of Saunders's friends to meet the next morning and start the campaign. Among them, Leslie Stratton and Cliff Blackburn both volunteered to help their former partner in his crisis.

The chamber organized a committee to handle the financial affairs of the stock sale drive. The committee—including Robert Leedy Matthews, a Piggly Wiggly Stores, Inc., board member, and John P. Bullington, a

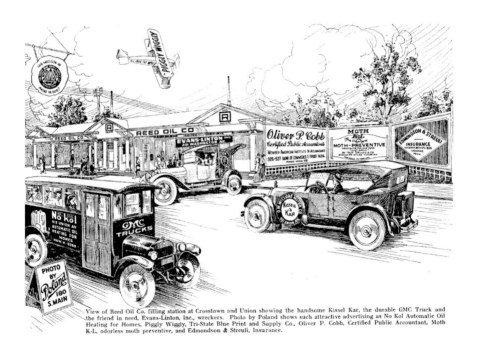

View of Reed Oil Co. filling station at Crosstown and Union showing the handsome Kissel Kar, the durable GMC Truck and the friend in need, Evans-Linton, Inc., wreckers. Photo by Poland shows such attractive advertising as No Kol Automatic Oil Heating for Homes, Piggly Wiggly, Tri-State Blue Print and Supply Co., Oliver P. Cobb, Certified Public Accountant, Moth K-L, odorless moth preventive, and Edmondson & Streuli, Insurance.

Piggly Wiggly also promoted a national image for Memphis, as Coca-Cola had done for Atlanta, Georgia, according to the chamber of commerce. This advertisement in the 1923 *Journal* played upon Saunders's fascination with airplanes. *Courtesy of Special Collections, McWherter Library, University of Memphis.*

Memphis investor, who also sold Saunders the land for his unfinished estate—were to collect and hold all money subscribed in trust. This committee would select accountants to investigate conditions of Piggly Wiggly Stores, Inc., both before and after stock was issued to purchasers. It would then apply the funds to pay obligations of the Stores Company. Saunders was to supply shares of stock as collateral for the bank notes and loan agreements. If the committee discovered that all conditions of the drive were not met by the Stores Company, it would return all the money subscribed.

Saunders made amends to a potential enemy, Robert Snowden of the Bank of Commerce and Trust. On Thursday, May 3, Saunders announced he would give up his lease within the old Peabody Hotel and open his new Variety Store across Main Street. Free now to build his new Peabody Hotel, Snowden gave his approval to the stock sale drive. Snowden, incidentally, completed his new hotel in 1925; it is still a Memphis landmark. The newspapers on Friday, May 4, provided free advertising for the stock sale drive. In one ad, Joseph Fly of the Bowers Stores expressed his thoughts:

> *Absolutely square in his dealings with competitor, customer and business associate, Saunders is too big an asset for this community to lose, or to allow to be crushed by any combine in Wall Street or elsewhere… Mr. Saunders is a foeman worthy of any man's steel. When he fights he fights in the open. He is above board in all his dealings. He is every inch a man. We hope he comes through and places his stock right here in Memphis. However, engaging Wall Street in battle is too big a task for the greatest of generals to undertake alone. He must have the soldiers to back him.*

This ad impressed the editors of *Advertising Age* magazine with the esteem held by Saunders in Memphis. Even grocery rivals were helping him sell Piggly Wiggly stock.

The chamber created a new slogan for May 4, the last working day before the drive began: "Clarence Saunders is not broke until Memphis is broke." Under Leslie Stratton's direction, they organized twenty-eight sales committees along business lines. The *Commercial Appeal* pressmen and type operators, heading the publicity committees, helped string banners,

"Save Piggly Wiggly for Memphis," across downtown streets. Streamers with the slogan were placed on cars and placards in storefronts. Motion picture houses placed serials in their news segments urging patrons to join the cause. The American Legion, the Lions Club, the Kiwanis, the garden clubs, the railroad unions, schoolteachers, firemen, doctors, dentists and clergymen all pledged to buy stock. Saunders was touched. "I am proud and happy to be a Memphian," he returned the compliments, calling Joseph Fly and others "proof Memphians are fair and unselfish."

The campaigners touted the economic impact on the city by the Piggly Wiggly business. It employed over 250 people in Memphis, with a yearly payroll of $500,000. It rented over 60 buildings in Memphis and bought most of its supplies from Memphis companies. Of the now 1,267 Piggly Wiggly stores, 667 were owned by Piggly Wiggly Stores, Inc., with 50 of them in Memphis. The other stores were owned by franchisees, who paid a license fee and royalties to the parent corporation. Both the corporation and the Stores Company deposited most of its income in Memphis banks, which helped give Memphis the largest bank clearings of any southern city. Piggly Wiggly was a good investment; sales and earnings were increasing every year. The Piggly Wiggly Stores, Inc., common stock had paid dividends of 11 percent to investors. Piggly Wiggly also brought considerable revenue to other Memphis enterprises. Bill Donelson remembered that his father's wholesale grocery company brokered an order of canned milk for Piggly Wiggly. The volume of the purchase was fifty railroad cars.

Stratton picked fifty of the best salesmen to lead the stock drive. After an enthusiastic pep talk Monday morning, May 7, they hit the streets. Wearing buttons that said "Memphis 100% for Piggly Wiggly" and carrying subscription blanks, they literally called upon everybody. The first day's sales were promising. The campaigners celebrated with a rally that evening at the Hotel Gayoso. Saunders offered words of encouragement. Representatives from the pool of investors addressed the rally in turn. Lynn Dinkins of New Orleans reminded them that he was once a Memphian and they could be proud of their efforts on behalf of Piggly Wiggly.

It looked as if Clarence Saunders had at last solved his dilemma with Piggly Wiggly stock and could go back to managing the business. But that night, he inadvertently destroyed the stock sale campaign.

An English stonemason had injured himself while installing pink outer masonry on his new estate. The discovery of the accident must have stunned the stock sale leaders. Here was Saunders still spending money on that expensive house while many of them were working without pay to save his business. He was quick to placate them: "I will nail the place up, lock the gates and leave it until I can make money to lease it." But his words were not enough. In an instant, the salesmen's confidence had vanished. The incident unleashed a storm of criticism about the way he handled his business affairs. His detractors, many of them the bankers, accused him of running a one-man show. Piggly Wiggly's money was not managed properly, so the stock was not worth fifty-five dollars, despite popular sentiment.

The people of Clarksville were still proud of him, their native son. On June 5, 1923, he gave the commencement address at Southwestern Presbyterian University. Afterward, he and Carolyn were fêted by the Kiwanis Club. *Courtesy of Special Collections, McWherter Library, University of Memphis.*

Saunders "threw a bombshell into the ranks" of the campaign workers at the banquet Tuesday, May 8, by threatening to resign from Piggly Wiggly. He didn't want to make himself a distraction that might hinder the stock sale. He blamed his problems on the bankers who didn't like him. "They made me give up a valuable lease of the Peabody Hotel, but what have they done? Not one thing. Now they insist Clarence Saunders step down and let someone else manage the Piggly Wiggly campaign and they will put it over."

Friends of Saunders negotiated throughout Wednesday, May 9, to arrange a compromise. The bankers seemed to be inclined to help if Piggly Wiggly was managed by a committee with shared authority to advise Saunders. Walter Smith, R.A. Wilson of the St. Louis pool, Lynn Dinkins and R.A. Shillingslaw of Nashville were appointed to this new committee. Smith, as the committee chairman, acted to calm everyone. "Saunders is in the hands of friends now. There will be no more talk of his resignation," he said at the banquet that night.

There, all the pool members expressed confidence in Saunders. Rogers Caldwell jested that he would take Saunders back to Nashville and sell all the stock there. "The stock sale is still on…we must not let pessimism sway us," Stratton encouraged the campaigners. Indeed, more than half of the shares were pledged on Monday, the first day of the drive. Ernest Bradford arrived from Washington to remind banquet guests, "There is still magic in Clarence Saunders' name."

The committee members, bankers and financiers, were to have broad powers in the management of the Piggly Wiggly Stores. If the committee was to be successful, Saunders must allow them to share these powers— specifically, to manage finances and appoint people to the board of directors. After agreeing to the compromise, Saunders evidently balked. He refused to allow an audit of the company books.

The Memphis bankers then refused to support the stock sale. Thursday morning, May 10, the campaign leaders and the pool members held a meeting at the chamber of commerce headquarters. The meeting was a tense affair. Saunders and several men exchanged hot words, and then a pushing and shoving brawl erupted between Saunders and Robert Ellis. A tired and disappointed Stratton announced to the campaigners at the banquet Thursday night that there would be no more rallies and banquets.

The stock sale campaign was finished. Rumors flew about the city that Saunders was to be ousted from Piggly Wiggly or that Saunders was to move the business to Atlanta. Reportedly, he was invited to that city by its chamber of commerce.

Saunders made his announcement, "Memphis has fizzled!" implying that his adopted hometown had failed him. He was never quite able to admit that his own poor judgment spoiled the campaign. Once doubt was cast upon him, he would find it a harder struggle to save Piggly Wiggly. His friends at the *Commercial Appeal* tersely said, "Saunders is practically on his own now."

Saunders left town, but not for Atlanta. Quietly, he took a train to Clarksville. Joseph Boillin had a plan. Boillin realized that Henry Ford had successfully fought a three-year battle with Wall Street financiers for control of Ford Motor Company. Ford now enjoyed a cash surplus estimated at $153 million. Ford might use some of that money to bail Saunders out. Go to Michigan to see Ford, Boillin advised his former protégé. He arranged for Luke Lea, editor of the *Nashville Tennessean*, and Governor Peay to meet Saunders at Bowling Green, Kentucky, to travel to Detroit. Saunders was skeptical. He told his companions the trip was a "wild goose chase." "It was well known," he said, "Ford did not like to deal with stockholders." He relented to his friends and boarded the train. Still plagued with doubts, he left them at Louisville and spent the night in that city. Governor Peay and Lea continued to Detroit, where they were told Henry Ford was too busy to see the governor of Tennessee.

Before the trip, Saunders had arranged for businessmen from Chicago to meet with him Monday, May 14. That day, he announced his own plan to raise money for Piggly Wiggly. Admitting he had over-expanded in the past, he said, it was time now to trim back the size of the business until pressing debts were paid. Almost all the units of the Stores Company were offered for sale except for those in the Memphis area, the Variety Stores and a few other selected stores. He would conduct negotiations only in his office with transactions in cash, payable within ten days. The National Tea Company of Chicago bought the ninety-seven Chicago stores on May 15 for $1,500,000. News of the sale traveled quickly. Businessmen from Dallas, Fort Worth, San Antonio, Denver and Kansas City filled Saunders's office, all eager to buy Piggly Wiggly stores at discount prices. Saunders expected the pool members to be pleased with his fundraising efforts to repay their loans.

But the New Orleans and Nashville investors were not pleased. The previous week, Saunders, in a shouting match with Dinkins, demanded his resignation from his advisory position with the Piggly Wiggly Stores, Inc. The investors arrived in Memphis determined after the Chicago sale to stop him from divesting the assets of the company. They threatened Saunders with an injunction if he did not voluntarily halt store sale negotiations. Saunders insisted he would continue the sales, asking them to extend their loans to July 1. In another angry exchange on May 18, Dinkins stormed out of his office after Saunders refused to supply him with a list of stockholders. That day, the investors seized ninety-one thousand shares of stock used as collateral for the loans.

This instigated rumors that Saunders would be forced out in a takeover bid led by Lynn Dinkins.

Saunders called the actions unfair. "The hostile pool groups…were more hateful and spiteful than Wall Street because they didn't get the profits due them. Now they want to get rid of me."

That week was the most trying time yet. During the crisis, Saunders fitfully slept and missed meals. Still, for all appearances he was ever the optimist, confident of success. He laughed at suggestions that he rest more and take a vacation. The Clarksville trip was not a rest. He didn't need one, he said. Friends admired his courage and how well he seemed to bear the strain. "If the triumph over Wall Street turned out to be a phyrric victory, he set about in his own way to make good to his friends and backers. He was not daunted. He admits it has been a thorny patch but he has never lost his smile."

Saunders revealed his frustration once through verse in *The Turnstile*: "Fate served me meanly, but I looked at her and laughed That none

Memphians drove by the Pink Palace and wondered, "Why would he build something so big for just one family?" Saunders never finished the house. The completed Pink Palace became the city's first museum in 1930. *Courtesy of Special Collections, McWherter Library, University of Memphis.*

might know how bitter was the cup I quaffed Along came Joy and paused beside me where I sat Saying 'I came to see what you were laughing at.'"

Determined as he was to hide his feelings, his erratic behavior betrayed him. The Clarksville and Nashville friends who observed him on that weekend trip to meet Ford kept their thoughts to themselves. Many years later, he revealed that he took up to five hot baths a night while hashing out his problems. This only hints at the stress his family endured.

Still his friends worked for him, conferring with the hostile investors for a solution to the dispute. He was ready to concede something to his opposition. "This is my business," he told them, and "I know how to run it. I am the only one who can get you out. But you must give me time and you must not tie my hands. Extend those obligations until September 1 and January 1, 1924 and I will get you out. If I don't, then you can step in and take the business." They accepted his compromise proposal with one stipulation: Saunders must accept Dinkins's advisory position.

Despite the wishes of his advisors, he sold store units in Kansas City, Denver and San Antonio. All together, his transactions earned the barren treasury $2,500,000. The new cash infusion did not save Piggly Wiggly from the first business decline in its short history. Some of the companies supplying the Piggly Wiggly stores demanded "COD only." Favorite brands began to disappear from the shelves of the stores. A sharp cut in advertising had been made, and this in turn caused business to fall off still more.

On August 10, Saunders went to the governor's office to face Governor Peay, Luke Lea and Rogers Caldwell. Caldwell delivered the bad news: "Piggly Wiggly cannot be saved until you resign and let someone else run the company." Some of the loyal Memphis investors proposed that Saunders temporarily resign as president of the Piggly Wiggly Stores, Inc., at the same time that the pool members would accept the collateral stock at fifty dollars a share from him instead of cash. The New Orleans pool insisted, "Saunders must go!" They would no longer compromise with him.

Saunders sensed the inevitable. Hoping to stem confusion, he sent telegrams to all Piggly Wiggly employees asking them to remain on the job regardless of what happened to him. He said to the press about his troubles with the investors, "I am not bitter about it as I realize that is the fortunes of war…Wall Street has had its revenge…I have lost my money and my business as a result of the treachery practiced upon me by the New York Stock Exchange."

He resigned on Monday, August 13, along with Fletcher Scott from the board of directors of Piggly Wiggly Stores, Inc. John Bullington and coffee merchant Joseph Maury, another Memphis investor, replaced the departing board members. Robert Jordan, also defecting from Saunders's ranks of loyal supporters, filled Scott's position as vice-president.

John C. Bradford of Nashville was selected the new president of the company over Lynn Dinkins's objections. Bradford was a thirty-year-old insurance salesman with connections to Caldwell's American National Bank. He would eventually create a successful investment firm. For the job of running a grocery business, he was unprepared. He admitted to a Nashville paper that he had never even shopped at Piggly Wiggly. His function was to watch Piggly Wiggly for Caldwell and Co.

This fact absolutely galled Clarence Saunders. Greedy Caldwell was out to milk Piggly Wiggly for all it was worth, Saunders wrote in an open letter to all stockholders. "They thought it would be fine to hear their names mentioned as president of the company." Even worse, Saunders charged that they didn't know how to run the business. They would take over even if the business was ruined. The Nashville group did not care about the welfare of other stockholders, he warned. They did not know nor care about the sacrifice he and his loyal friends had endured to create Piggly Wiggly in the first place. During his first day at the Piggly Wiggly office, Bradford offered his hand to the ex-president, who was busy sorting his personal effects. Saunders refused to acknowledge the young man's presence.

To prevent a forced bankruptcy, Saunders turned over to the new directors of the Piggly Wiggly Stores, Inc., assets he valued at $9 million. Included in his assets were 125,000 shares of stock he estimated to be worth $5 million, even after depreciation. He also handed to them cash—$200,000 of it in Memphis banks, $500,000 from elsewhere. In a fit of defiance, he emptied the change from his pockets. It was expected he would be forced to surrender his Cla-Le-Clare estate—estimated to be worth $875,000—his current home on Central valued at $212,000 and a number of automobiles. Afterward, he spoke eloquently: "I've got to get a job, to eat...I am forced to begin where I did when I left my grocery business to establish Piggly Wiggly...I have turned over everything I own...they have it all, everything I built, the greatest stores of their kind in the world; but they didn't get the man that was the father to the idea. They have the body of Piggly Wiggly but they didn't get the soul."

Chapter 7
Piggly Wiggly v. Saunders

Men I sought to protect broke me.

S aunders, still president of the Piggly Wiggly Corporation, tried to
save his position with that company. He wrote to the stockholders of
the parent company asking for half of their shares. He proposed to sell
these and use the money to pay off Caldwell. He called two meetings on
Friday, August 17, with the board of directors. The first meeting was not
successful for him. The stockholders who attended were not going to help
him fight Caldwell. "Now don't you do something in the meantime,"
some of the directors warned him. Saunders did exactly that, filing suit
against the directors of Piggly Wiggly. He, Fletcher Scott and Chester
Walker then resigned from the corporation board.

During the second meeting, the remaining directors appointed John
Bullington vice-president; Ewing W. Rollow of Clarksville secretary-
treasurer; Walter Smith's brother and business partner, Charles D. Smith,
president of the Piggly Wiggly Corporation.

Again Saunders watched former allies turn against him. Rollow
had worked for Boillin-Hurst along with Saunders years before. His
promotion irritated Saunders. In public statements, he questioned
Rollow's competence, citing Rollow's failure to manage a franchise Piggly
Wiggly store. Joseph Maury and Piggly Wiggly lawyer William Fitzhugh
assumed positions on the board.

In his suit, Saunders petitioned that the court appoint a bankruptcy receiver to oversee the Piggly Wiggly Corporation. The Piggly Wiggly Corporation needed the protection of the court because it was now in the hands of men who would exploit it, he declared. In his opinion, both Piggly Wiggly companies were now in the hands of the same cartel of stockholders, essentially the Nashville, New Orleans and St. Louis investors. Many of these men had profited at his expense during the stock market transactions by demanding high commission fees and interest rates for loans. Now they were ready to extract profits from Piggly Wiggly at the expense of the other stockholders. The men recently appointed to manage the companies were not experienced or competent in the grocery business. Saunders repeated his arguments for the court action in his letters to Piggly Wiggly stockholders and to the newspapers.

The directors of Piggly Wiggly claimed they did not need a court-appointed receiver. On August 22, Bullington, acting for the corporation, filed a countersuit in federal court. The corporation demanded from Saunders's Piggly Wiggly Investment Company an accounting of the stock bought the previous spring. They insisted the court prohibit Saunders from disposing of any money received from the stock sales. The corporation charged that the investment company's books did not show which stock belonged to Saunders and which to the Piggly Wiggly Corporation. The books did not show what price the stock sold for or whether there were any shares left in the corporation treasury during a recent audit. The corporation alleged that Saunders sold stock and kept that money with him. The suit demanded that Saunders repay that money, which they estimated at $2 million.

Saunders answered the corporation the next day by reentering his suit in federal court, demanding that the corporation pay him $2,316,947. He claimed he spent as much of his personal wealth on stock transactions for the corporation or on loans from the stockholders and directors. In his suit, he listed as an asset of the corporation his proposed lawsuit against the New York Stock Exchange for claims of over $5 million. At the moment, Saunders insisted, the corporation was not able to pay back its debts, totaling over $1 million to creditors.

Federal Judge John Ross on August 24 refused to dismiss the bankruptcy suits as requested by the Piggly Wiggly officials. He appointed lawyer Clarence Marsilliot to determine if the Piggly Wiggly Corporation was actually insolvent, as Saunders had claimed. Marsilliot, using his authority as the bankruptcy standing master, simplified the dispute by combining the opposing lawsuits into one.

During the first session of court, William Fitzhugh questioned the former president's sincerity. He asked Saunders why he waited until after the corporation filed a claim for over $2 million against him to file his own claim of over $2 million against the corporation. "What are you insinuating, Mr. Fitzhugh?" Saunders shouted at the witness stand. Marsilliot stood between the two men until order prevailed. (A family legend has Saunders hitting a bankruptcy referee, but this story has not been verified.) Later in the session, Saunders more calmly described the stock market transactions that led to the corner and the present lawsuit. Previously, the Hudson Trust Company of New York had put 1,500 shares of Stores Company stock up for public auction. The stock was held by the bank as collateral for a $30,000 loan. An unknown bidder purchased the stock for $1 a share. In court, Fitzhugh asked Saunders why he did not warn the new officers of the corporation about the loan due the Hudson Trust Company. Perhaps they could have protected the shares from the embarrassing junk stock sale. The Hudson loan was one of many loans, Saunders replied. He did not believe the corporation was able to cover many of them.

Court testimony did not resume until September 18. On that date, Clarence Saunders watched his benefactor, Joseph Boillin, testify against him. Boillin recalled how he had once given young Saunders a chance in the wholesale grocery business twenty-five years before and how Saunders, after making a fortune with Piggly Wiggly, in turn gave him a chance to share in the profits. Boillin now claimed that Saunders had recently misused his powers as the corporation's president. Once before, in April 1922, the corporation board had given Saunders unlimited authority to trade in Piggly Wiggly stocks, at that time a new issue of fifty thousand shares of Stores Company stock. The board, he asserted, could not anticipate the stock transactions Saunders would make one year later leading to the attempted corner.

Lovick Miles, Saunders's principal attorney, grilled Boillin in cross-examination. He forced Boillin to admit that the corporation board never revoked its decision of April 1922. Miles, therefore, argued that Saunders, as corporate president, had the authority to trade Piggly Wiggly stocks as he wished. Miles skillfully laid bare the corporation directors' attempts to masquerade as innocent victims of Saunders. On the contrary, they knew exactly what Saunders was attempting when he cornered Piggly Wiggly stock. Boillin recruited Nashville businessmen to invest in the corner activities. Quickly, Fitzhugh put Boillin back on the stand. Of course, Boillin conceded, everyone within the corporation knew Saunders was trying to corner Piggly Wiggly. But all believed Saunders was acting for himself and not as an agent of the corporation.

The next witness, Rogers Caldwell, repeated the corporation defense, insisting that Saunders acted on his own. Miles forced Caldwell to admit he made $100,000 on his loan to the corporation. On September 19, Fitzhugh tried to attack Saunders from a different perspective, introducing evidence on Saunders's unfinished estate, Cla-Le-Clare.

Two New Orleans financial institutions associated with Lynn Dinkins filed another suit against Saunders to collect $84,750. They claimed this was the amount due in commission from Saunders for arranging loans totaling $1,250,000. The number of legal actions involved became too confusing for Judge Ross. He ordered that the prosecution of all suits in connection with Saunders and Piggly Wiggly be stopped until the receivership issue was settled. However, he also announced all holders of loans to Saunders over $150,000 were entitled to be part of the receivership suit, giving Dinkins and the New Orleans pool what they wanted.

The corporation officials were themselves discouraged with the legal problems. The publicity surrounding the court case had damaged Piggly Wiggly's reputation and market value. Their stock was vulnerable to other predatory speculators, like the buyer at the Hudson auction. Judge Ross agreed. He placed 28,500 shares of Stores Company stock, used by Saunders as collateral for loans, under a receiver, Thomas King. King was ordered to guard the shares (valued in the spring of 1923 at $1,500,000) against quick sale at a loss of value by either side. Their fears seemed to come true in November when New York brokers specializing in junk stock sale sent letters to stockholders offering to buy Piggly Wiggly stock at $11 and $15 a share. The corporation made its complaint again. These dealers were frightening the small stockholder, who could not afford to lose, into unloading the stock at a loss. Marsilliot threatened the dealers with prosecution if they did not stop this practice.

The Piggly Wiggly receivership case proved to be a difficult and complicated decision. Five months later, on Friday, February 22, 1924,

Lovick Miles pressed for a quick decision in the case. Marsilliot literally threw up his hands. Such a case, he said, would take at least four or five additional months of concentrated labor. Searching through the documents was tedious; there were at least five hundred pages of financial audits alone to read. The job was made more difficult because of the inaccurate records kept by Saunders and the corporation. Some things pertinent to the case were not documented at all, explained the bankruptcy master. He asked Judge Ross for assistance in compiling the court documents. Ross assessed both parties $15,000 for court costs. The attorneys for both parties complained futilely.

For Saunders, the new bond meant an unpleasant decision. He had no money to pay it. He could no longer make the payment on his Central Avenue home nor maintain the lifestyle he had grown accustomed to. Late Saturday evening, February 23, Miles filed for him a voluntary petition of bankruptcy. Saunders and his family moved out of their home to the Parkview Hotel. This move did not lower their standard of living much. The Parkview was the most expensive rental in Memphis, paid for by Carolyn's savings. Judge Marsilliot appointed John W. Canada trustee of Saunders's estate. Saunders revealed his plans. "For six months I have been in court with no business and no income…I must make a living. I will open up a new store in fifty days. My new chain of stores will be just as big a success as my first creation, Piggly Wiggly."

Fletcher Scott, Chester Walker, and Carolyn immediately gave him $12,000 to start the new business. He hired the same crew that had built his first Piggly Wiggly eight years before to create his new store at Third and Madison. He filed a patent application on its design. He promised a grand opening on March 8, reminiscent of Piggly Wiggly's grand opening with jazz music and free carnations for all visitors. He named his new store after himself, the "Clarence Saunders Self-Service Store." Soon he announced that he would sell franchises and issues of stock. Saunders wanted to issue fifty thousand shares of common stock and ten thousand shares of preferred stock in his new licensing company, the Clarence Saunders Corporation. In the midst of all his plans, Saunders became reflective: "Today I have the experience of years in back of me…I have no expectations of ever being connected with Piggly Wiggly again…There is no doubt there is room in the self-service field for both myself and other chain systems. I am not going to operate the system to destroy or tear down."

The directors of the Piggly Wiggly Corporation did not trust Saunders. They presented their complaints to Judge Ross on March 6. They accused Saunders of spreading rumors that Piggly Wiggly was to close down stores and that he encouraged employees to quit the company. Their other argument was that Clarence Saunders was still under contract to the Piggly Wiggly Corporation. The contracts stipulated he could not patent any self-service arrangements or fixtures for himself or another company. He could not use any fixtures and equipment that infringed upon the corporation's patent rights. Saunders's new store and patent application, in their opinion, violated the contracts. He was also infringing upon their trademark and copyrights. His name was inevitably linked in the public mind with self-service and the name "Piggly Wiggly." The contracts gave to the corporation the right to the business goodwill of his name. How easy it would be for Clarence Saunders to promote his new business as the creator and ex-president of Piggly Wiggly. It was unfair to the Piggly Wiggly stockholders for Clarence Saunders to take advantage of his past association while operating a competing grocery chain. Truly, they feared for their market position if Saunders were allowed to compete against Piggly Wiggly.

An odd battle was now being waged in the federal courts in this new round of *Piggly Wiggly v. Saunders*. The Piggly Wiggly Corporation asked for protection of its trademark and patent rights against the very man who created and sold those rights to the corporation. The corporation, in attempting to block Saunders from opening a new grocery store, paid an ironic compliment to his great merchandising accomplishments. Judge Ross was perplexed by the case. He ordered an injunction preventing Clarence Saunders from opening his store for ten days. Then he would decide on the infringement issues.

Saunders's lawyers argued in vain. He had not led Piggly Wiggly employees away from their jobs. Some old friends, Rueben Harris among them, left Piggly Wiggly, but they quit of their own accord. They denied he would take advantage of his position as ex-president of Piggly Wiggly for advertising purposes. John Farley, the patent attorney who witnessed many of his earlier patent applications, also testified for Saunders. He stated that the store arrangements, advertising, color schemes and fixtures were very different from that of Piggly Wiggly. Lovick Miles argued that one could not deny him the use of his own name, just because he was so well known. That was as ridiculous as denying Theodore Roosevelt the right to his name. And if Saunders could not use his name, then it was impossible for him to sell franchise licenses, a potentially great loss to him.

Saunders was discouraged by the injunction but not surprised. In his advertisement on March 6, he wrote of those who wanted him to fail—who "stabbed me in the back." He promised to open his new store someday, but not for those people. "No, he would do it for…the throng of unafraid and confident men and women who…believed in me." Saunders stood in the doorway of his locked store, his children by his side, and handed out carnations until he ran out of flowers.

Clarence Saunders had to change the mind of Judge Ross. "I Am the Sole Owner of This Name!" he shouted Sunday, March 9, in his advertisement in the *Appeal.* He tried to distance his name from identification with Piggly Wiggly, using examples of his Piggly Wiggly ads and copyrighted material that did not publish his name. His enemies at Piggly Wiggly would not stop him from opening a self-service grocery, for he wrote, they do not have exclusive rights to self-service. And, he admitted, other grocery men used self-service before he did in 1916.

He renounced his creative work with Piggly Wiggly. His new store did not need a turnstile or a forced passageway. Self-service was so common now that the patents were virtually useless. *Courtesy of the Memphis Room, Memphis Public Library and Information Center.*

At last, March 28, the end of the injunction was near. Saunders was excited. In his advertisement;, "Full Steam! Ready!" he took the opportunity to thank his supporters:

> *Right here in Memphis, the place that I love above all other towns or cities, is where I am happy to start again the foundation of another great business. To every corner of the earth I shall endeavor to spread the good qualities and their fame of the Memphis people, and in your midst I shall continue to take my troubles as they come and I share with you all the good things that I may receive.*

It was a relief to be back in business again and have the injunction case finished—or so it seemed.

Judge Ross let him down again. Citing the complex legal briefs submitted by both sides, he extended the injunction for the third time. Visibly shaken, Saunders called Judge Ross unfair and insisted he would open Saturday in spite of the injunction.

Saunders was also in court to face his new bankruptcy referee, Charles Thompson. His creditors, positive he had disposed of some of his assets before declaring bankruptcy, were upset with Saunders. They had not found any of Saunders's autos or airplanes on the estate properties. Saunders resented their accusations. They also discussed the sale of the estate properties. The trustee's real estate agents appraised the Central Avenue property at $75,000 and the Pink Palace at $400,000. Saunders listened to his creditors in the courtroom. Asked if it bothered him to watch others divide and label his belongings, he replied, "I have lost interest. I don't care for wealth or splendor…only to be building something of big proportions."

Kit Williams, a young associate of Guston Fitzhugh, traveled on Friday night, March 29, to the home of Judge Ross in Jackson. There he beseeched the judge to relent and lift Saunders's injunction. Ross decided to send the case to the Circuit Court of Appeals. In the interim, he allowed Saunders to open for business, warning Saunders not to infringe on Piggly Wiggly's rights.

Saunders waited inside his store the entire night without sleep for the judge's decision. Saturday, March 30, he opened the doors of the first Clarence Saunders, Sole Owner of My Name Store. Saunders again

Location of this photo is unknown. But the crowd at Third and Madison looked similar to this. "We're with you, Mr. Saunders!" they said. That day he stood without rest for ten hours. *Courtesy of the Memphis Room, Memphis Public Library and Information Center.*

stood at the entrance giving flowers, a handshake and smiles to the thousands of visitors. One of the people in line was a federal marshal who, on this visit, had no court order. Saunders handed him a bouquet of carnations. From on top of an icebox a syncopating jazz orchestra played "When I Get You Alone" and other hit tunes. Saunders was triumphant. He later wrote of the grand opening, "The charm of it all, the lasting memory that I shall keep of that day is the refreshing fragrance of life." Saunders had plenty of bitterness left for his legal adversaries. In the same advertisement, he wrote: "I have cut out of my desire and thoughts every former affection that I had for Piggly Wiggly. To me now the word is obnoxious, and so much so if every Piggly Wiggly store was offered to me as a gift plus $1,000,000 in cash, I would refuse to accept…This is my Monday washing and I am done."

Chapter 8
THE SOLE OWNER MAN

A man is not a failure as long as he keeps trying.

"Oh You Bumble! Listen to the bumble of the bumble bee when the sun gets too hot," he warbled in his ad on June 28. Saunders had reason to cheer; he had already opened four Sole Owner stores. The competition in the grocery business in 1924 was unlike the old-fashioned grocery stores of eight years before. In Memphis, many chain grocery stores competed with Piggly Wiggly and Mr. Bowers. Most of these chains utilized self-service. All touted their advantages to shoppers in full- or half-page newspaper ads. Technology also changed: more advanced refrigeration equipment allowed grocers to display delicate, perishable foods. Once scarce luxuries were now being offered for sale every day.

Saunders entered the competition again by offering a greater variety of food and providing, of all things, a return to clerk service. A Mr. Bowers spokesman could not resist the opportunity to rebuke Saunders for his seemingly inconsistent behavior. "Others...change policies overnight. The strongest advocate of self-service has been converted...to service." Saunders was too clever to bind himself to a static policy in the face of consumer demands.

Saunders found ways to retaliate against his competition. He waited until the last minute, late Thursday night, to place his advertisement for the Friday paper. The *Commercial Appeal* gave to him privileges denied other advertisers, such as allowing him to proofread his own copy. The

The Sole Owner Store was larger than a Piggly Wiggly. He had arranged the store for both self-service and clerk service. Clerks served customers in the butcher, bakery and deli departments. *Courtesy of Special Collections, McWherter Library, University of Memphis.*

newspaper hired extra linotype operators for the larger Friday edition. Saunders tipped each man ten dollars, more than their daily wage. Casually he glanced at the ads run by his competitors. The other chain stores complained to the newspaper advertising office: "Saunders is taking advantage of his last minute placement. He can see what we are charging for our prices and change his." To quiet criticism, the newspaper moved its deadline for advertisement placement to Wednesday. Saunders used new tactics. In one ad, a figure drawing of "Sole Owner" is depicted firing a cannon at targets "Piggly Wiggly," "Mr. Bowers" and "Arrow Stores." By September, he had expanded to seven stores.

That good news could not offset his legal predicament. On August 20, one year after he resigned from Piggly Wiggly, the corporation gained a victory in its suit against him. Bankruptcy master Clarence Marsilliot ruled that the Piggly Wiggly Corporation was solvent and did not need a bankruptcy receiver, as Saunders had demanded. Instead, he ruled that the former head of the corporation owed Piggly Wiggly a total of $2,529,000. In his 239-page decision, Marsilliot carefully explained how Saunders incurred that debt. He conceded that Clarence Saunders was a genius but also an eccentric, intimidating man to work with: "Because of the fact he had brought the whole enterprise into being and managed it with almost startling success, it is clear from this record that Saunders found himself unable to bear in mind he was not dealing with his own property."

Marsilliot's most damning criticism involved the expenditure of $308,194 of Piggly Wiggly corporate accounts by President Saunders to build the Pink Palace. Marsilliot also assumed that Saunders used some of the money loaned to him by the pool interests for his personal accounts instead of for corner transactions. But the personal records and the bookkeeping of Clarence Saunders were sometimes so confusing it was difficult for Marsilliot to tell which sums of money were corporate and which were personal. Marsilliot stopped short of accusing Saunders of fraudulent, criminal embezzlement. The directors of the company published excerpts of his opinion in two full-page ads to exonerate themselves of the stock market disaster. For a year, the public had listened to Saunders talk of a "conspiracy" by the board of directors to bankrupt and defraud him of his Piggly Wiggly. Here was proof that Clarence Saunders's statements were false.

Truth and falsehood in a dispute such as this was a matter of interpretation, Saunders replied: "As to who is going to be proved the liar in the end is yet to be determined." He felt betrayed once again by his former friends at Piggly Wiggly. They had totally convinced Marsilliot of their side of the story. He felt Marsilliot was biased against him, and Saunders was thankful the bankruptcy master did not have the power to enforce his opinion.

Judge Ross held that power. Saunders surprised his opponents and Judge Ross when his lawyers filed suit accusing both Judge Ross and Marsilliot of bias. He compiled a list of slights and errors they committed during the long court proceedings. Saunders accused the judge of a conflict of interest because he owed money to Isaac Tigrett, a member of Caldwell's investor pool (who was also an early investor in Piggly

Wiggly, but Saunders did not mention that). His comments sparked rumors throughout the state. Judge Ross's good reputation was tarnished. The *Clarksville Leaf-Chronicle* said its hometown hero, Saunders, was too irresponsible in his remarks. The paper, which had recently admired his exploits, now complained that he indulged in too many sensational stunts. He had better find proof about Judge Ross or apologize.

Ross scoffed at Saunders's charges but gave Saunders precisely what he wanted: the judge excused himself from the case. When one party in a suit is convinced the judge is prejudiced, it is best to allow another judge to hear the case, he declared. Someone else would make the final decision in *Piggly Wiggly v. Saunders.*

To Saunders's dismay, Judge Smith Hickenlooper of the Cincinnati Federal Court confirmed Marsilliot's opinion on April 4, 1925. Judge Hickenlooper differed from Marsilliot in one important matter. The pool interests, he noted, were hardly innocent victims of Saunders's manipulations. Thus, they were not entitled to full compensation from Saunders in his debts to the Piggly Wiggly Corporation. Hickenlooper adjusted Saunders's debts to $1,664,203. The judge left open the question whether Saunders was obliged to pay the full amount of the debt.

Saunders was still under the bankruptcy guardianship of Charles Thompson, a fact that irritated him. In court a month later, Thompson was the victim of Saunders's wit. Thompson pressed Saunders about the valuable belongings he allegedly hid from the court. Saunders told the court about the occasion Thompson had borrowed his silver cocktail shaker and never returned it. "Where's my cocktail shaker?" he asked. Then he entertained the courtroom crowd with stories of the cocktail party, until Thompson ordered him to shut up. Flustered, Thompson demanded Saunders turn over his expensive household furniture. "Get it yourself! I'm not taking my wife's furniture away from her." The courtroom crowd cheered him, but they didn't make legal decisions, and Saunders was not released from bankruptcy.

The public did support Saunders's comeback in the grocery trade. The Sole Owner stores grew as rapidly as Saunders could find people to buy a franchise or manage a new store. It was most gratifying to see former Piggly Wiggly franchisees and employees rejoin him in business. The Wyatt family of Dallas quit their management of Piggly Wiggly to buy the Sole Owner franchise there. Milton Magnus, one of Saunders's

Dry Agents Tie And Abuse H

500 Millions at 60, is Hope Of Clarence Saunders; Tells Of Comeback in Big Business

Undaunted at 47, after being busted by Wall street.

Fort Worth, Tex., Sept. 19. —Clarence Saunders, who lost his fortune and control of the Piggly-Wiggly stores two years ago in a spectacular Wall street battle, while here on Saturday explained how he expected to be worth $500,-000,000 when he is 60. His method is simple. He compels himself to be his own worst competitor.

Saunders is 47 and except for graying hair still has the appearance and vigor of youth. He visited Fort Worth to attend the opening of his 60th store.

"My loss in Wall street was the best thing that ever happened to me," he said. "For I have learned how to think, how to look ahead and how to analyze the other fellow. Formerly I took it for granted the other fellow would adopt an attitude similar to mine. Now I know all men are different and I learn this difference with all men I deal with

His worst competitor.

CLARENCE SAUNDERS.

boxing, golfing, dancing and politics. he has turned philosopher—of the rapid-fire type.

In city after city, newspapers reported of his comeback. The *Buffalo News* reported a wire service story of Saunders at the grand opening of his Fort Worth stores. *Courtesy of Special Collections, McWherter Library, University of Memphis.*

favored salesmen, bought the rights for Birmingham, Alabama. Saunders traveled to the city himself to take part in the grand opening of the Sole Owner Stores. Another ex–Piggly Wiggly man operated the Jackson, Mississippi store.

His employees remembered Clarence Saunders as having an inexhaustible energy. Physically strong as ever, he often worked from sunrise until late evening. Employees had to work as many hours as he did—six days a week (he always took Sunday off), twelve to fourteen hours a day, depending on the amount of business. Much of that time he spent in his stores soliciting his customers' opinions. Sometimes he and a crew worked all night preparing a new store for operation. His employees feared their boss's temper. He would stride into a store, entourage in tow, and finding something that displeased him, say a shelf in need of repair, command them to: "Tear out that shelving right now!" Those who disliked him did not stay employed with him very long.

Saunders's demands were not unusual; many employers expected long working hours from their staff. And many employees did not mind; fulfilling these demands was the way to get ahead in his business, of proving your mettle. One employee reported that some of his colleagues "worked themselves to an early grave."

Those who did like Saunders often remained steadfastly loyal to him. Mrs. Eva Johnson was his personal secretary for thirty-five years. He trusted her so much that he allowed her to fill out her paycheck with whatever amount she felt was appropriate. "He couldn't be bothered with the details," she insisted. Saunders took an interest in new employees with promise, cultivating their acquaintance. He paid at or above prevailing wages; a store manager earned $35.00 a week, a cashier $22.50 supplemented by bonuses and loans. He was fair in negotiations with the trade unions.

In July, Thompson announced that the creditors of the Saunders estate would launch their suit against the New York Stock Exchange over the corner transactions of 1922 and 1923. They sought to recover $2 million. Carruthers Ewing, who once represented Saunders against the Exchange, was retained as their legal counsel. Saunders refused to help his creditors in their suit. Saunders informed the "hated" Exchange that he would not help his former friends recoup the money they had lost from his corner transactions. It was another odd twist in the fight between Saunders and Piggly Wiggly.

Thompson sold the Pink Palace estate. After claims by suppliers and contractors were settled, the corporation received $228,969. The estate was purchased by the Gardens Community Corporation of Louisville, which developed the property into an exclusive subdivision, Chickasaw Gardens. In exchange for utilities construction, it deeded the house to the City of Memphis. The city, in turn, created Memphis's first public museum inside the Pink Palace. Finally, Saunders was released from bankruptcy on November 27, 1925, a thankful moment during the Thanksgiving holiday.

Judge John Gore of the Nashville Federal Court discharged most of the balance of Saunders's debts on December 16. Judge Gore differed sharply from Marsilliot and Hickenlooper in their assessment of the directors of Piggly Wiggly. They were not entitled at all to recover their money from Saunders lost during the corner. Nevertheless, Judge Gore did not absolve Saunders from all his debts to the Piggly Wiggly Corporation. Borrowing corporate funds for personal use and failing to repay was an act of embezzlement, the judge stated. The corporation was entitled to payments of roughly $201,000. Saunders was also liable for income taxes of approximately $100,000. He also criticized Saunders for his outrageous behavior during the trials. Saunders apologized to the court.

Both Saunders and the Piggly Wiggly Corporation were weary of litigation, and Judge Gore's decision cleared the way for a compromise. Saunders was to pay the corporation $150,000 over a two-year period. All litigation between the two parties would cease. His lawyers also negotiated with the Internal Revenue Service to reduce his tax bill. Thompson released money held in Saunders's bankruptcy trust to pay the bills. It seemed as if the New Year had brought Saunders's legal problems to a close.

Unfortunately, his difficulties with Piggly Wiggly were not quite finished. Rumors spread that the United States Post Office and the Justice Department were preparing to indict Clarence Saunders. The expected charge was mail fraud in the direct sale campaign of Piggly Wiggly stock in 1923. The statute of limitations was to expire soon. Federal investigators had visited Piggly Wiggly officials who, it was said, initiated the probe. Saunders was furious. He was convinced these corporation men, particularly John Burch, often impugned his honesty. All of Saunders's old animosities surfaced. Together with his bodyguard, Harry Light, they strode into the Exchange Building to the seventh-floor corporate office of Piggly Wiggly. Light guarded the door while his boss stepped inside John Burch's office and Saunders confronted the man, who rose to defend himself. He denied launching the investigation. Saunders hit him once, knocking him to the ground. A crowd of office employees rushed to the scene. Light fended them off, and the pair escaped. Someone called the police. Saunders was arrested on the ground floor of the building. Still fuming an hour later he said, "It has been freely talked about...they would get me yet."

Two weeks later, an indictment was imminent. Saunders felt sadder and bitterer about this than any part of the Piggly Wiggly stock corner epic. "Shame, Disgrace and Infamy" he titled one advertisement: "The whole infernal mess is brought about because of the great success of my new Saunders Sole Owner Stores in competition with Piggly Wiggly. They have tried every other way to ruin me and this is the meanest and vilest of all."

The federal grand jury issued its indictment on February 19. The indictment stemmed from Piggly Wiggly stockholders and officials in St. Louis, not Memphis. They alleged that in June 1923, Saunders, through mailers and circulars, promised a 7 percent return on investment in Stores Company stock. He had also promised to finance a new issue of stock. Of course, these promises were not fulfilled. Saunders by that time did not even have full control of the Stores Company stock. Instead, Saunders had used the invested money to pay the margin of stock he had already purchased or to pay off loans. The indictments carried a maximum penalty of five years' imprisonment and a $10,000 fine.

Saunders in his newspaper advertisement vowed to fight the indictment. And he apologized to John Burch: "I have done one thing that I regret in all of this mess of things, and that was my fistic encounter with John Burch…I now think I was mistaken as to the part he was taking in the affair."

Special Prosecutor Horace Dye and District Attorney Edward Murray were prepared to arrest and transfer him to St. Louis. Kit Williams and John Canada protested, in federal court, that the grand jury was incorrect in claiming Saunders had sent the letters offering Stores Company stock in June 1923. Those letters, they argued, were actually sent three months earlier, when Saunders still controlled the stock and still had some hope of saving his business from the corner debacle. The letters then were not an attempt to defraud. Judge Harry Anderson was sympathetic to their arguments. He ordered the district attorney not to arrest Clarence Saunders. His decision caught the prosecution by surprise. They never succeeded in bringing Saunders to trial. The indictment was dropped following the death of Horace Dye in July 1928.

Saunders's fight against Piggly Wiggly was, at last, at end. But he kept in his mind the memory of Rogers Caldwell at the governor's office with friends Luke Lea and Governor Austin Peay beside him, saying that he, Clarence Saunders, must give up his brainchild Piggly Wiggly.

By 1926, four years after his inauguration, Governor Peay had accomplished many of his goals, and on the whole he was a popular man in the state. He was indecisive about running for a third term in 1926. The governor was then fifty and suffering from a heart condition. He felt pressured by the tradition in American politics against third terms. Yet he feared if he retired from public office now, a new administration would dismantle his reforms. Governor Peay announced he would campaign for reelection in 1926, and as expected, he won endorsements from influential people across the state.

Saunders stunned Peay when he announced his support for the governor's chief opponent, Hill McAlister, in the August primary. On July 23, two weeks before the summer primary, Saunders announced, "I believe Austin Peay has been governor long enough. If he gets a third term, he or someone else will ask for a fourth or fifth term." In an advertisement that same day, Saunders attacked his friend as indifferent to the suffering of others. Then he contrasted his hard childhood with the governor's privileged youth.

He followed Peay's campaign maneuvers, searching for material to ridicule. The governor in his campaign remarks emphasized his religious faith. Saunders replied with this parody: "Lord, I thank Thee again and again that out of Tennessee's great sins You have raised me to the pinnacle of Thy Great I Am Ness." On August 4, Governor Peay mentioned the problems with his health. Saunders made fun of him with, "Really, we will all sob ourselves to death, Mr. Peay, if you don't quit talking about laying down your life for Tennessee."

The governor won the Democratic primary by eight thousand votes. Austin Peay, in public, never responded to Saunders's insults. Privately, he was wounded by them. Any politician expected harsh words from an enemy, but Saunders had been a friend. He believed that he had helped Saunders during his Piggly Wiggly troubles. Unfortunately, Saunders had proved once more that advertising was a potent tool—it can destroy a friendship.

On April 10, 1927, three years after he opened his first Sole Owner store, Clarence Saunders settled his last debt to the Piggly Wiggly Corporation. He wrote a check to the corporation for $80,600, which covered all payments and interest due. Saunders felt liberated at last. By then, he owned or leased 220 Sole Owner stores in 127 towns in 15 states. He estimated his 1927 total sales to be $25 million. His Clarence Saunders Corporation owned the Memphis stores outright. In 1927, the Saunders Corporation earned $200,000 in store sales and royalty and franchise fees, paying a dividend on the preferred and common stock. In Chicago during the month of March 1927, Saunders completed an agreement with investors in that city to form a new company, the Clarence Saunders Stores, Incorporated. The new company was to open 25 stores in Chicago as soon as store sites could be found and prepared.

Saunders wanted his grocery chain to expand nationally, at an even faster rate. He was near fulfilling his dreams of a second fortune and a business as great as Piggly Wiggly. He had already acquired a spacious home on Goodwyn Road and installed a swimming pool. The home lay across the narrow lane from the gate of the Memphis Country Club, only a block away from the Pink Palace.

In general, the public was glad Saunders had persevered through his myriad legal battles. Saunders encouraged people to accept these romantic notions of him. "I didn't waste time moaning about my losses on Wall Street," he announced to a group of accountants in Chicago. "I was just as happy two years ago when I was broke and owed $150,000 as I am today with more than $2,000,000."

Of course, Saunders's vindictive temper sometimes betrayed the public image he so carefully fostered. His insulting comments toward Austin Peay, for example, would haunt him. The governor never finished his third term. He died suddenly on October 2, 1927, of a cerebral hemorrhage. Saunders expressed shock and remorse over the death of Governor Austin Peay.

Chapter 9
SECOND FORTUNE

The dollar mark of profit...

The speaker of the state senate, Henry Horton, stepped in to complete Peay's unexpired term of office. In 1928, Governor Horton announced he would run for his own term. Governor Horton's chief opponent was Hill McAlister, endorsed in Memphis by Edward Crump. Clarence Saunders gave his allegiance to Governor Horton. Perhaps he felt guilty over his betrayal of Austin Peay two years before. The Horton election campaign would be his chance to make amends with the late governor's friends.

In Memphis, the candidates in this primary were overshadowed by their more celebrated supporters. Saunders opened his campaign efforts with a practical joke. In nearby Covington, Tennessee, Hill McAlister spoke to a rally attended by Crump and his organization. His speech was disrupted by two airplanes. Lee Saunders, twenty-two years old, and Clay Saunders, sixteen, flew over the rally, dropping leaflets reading "HORTON IS THE MAN CLARENCE SAUNDERS." The proud father discreetly watched from across the highway. He followed that stunt with gleeful prose: "Mr. Ed Crump Gets Mad! And the buzz of a little airplane did it. Now, I say, a man's got to be red-headed [Crump was well known in his youth for red hair] if he will get mad at a harmless little sporting around in the air."

The *Press-Scimitar* replied first, dismissing the airplanes as a foolish stunt. Then the paper questioned Saunders's political sincerity. After all, in 1926, the *Press-Scimitar*, Crump and Saunders had opposed the late Governor Peay's third-term bid; Saunders had even worked for the McAlister campaign against Governor Peay in 1926. Now Saunders opposed McAlister and insulted Crump. "Two-faced," the *Press-Scimitar* called him. Crump wrote newspaper ads calling Saunders a "fresh upstart," "squirt" and "smart-aleck." Hinting that Saunders owed money to Caldwell's banks, Crump reopened wounds and questioned Saunders's integrity:

> *He is the kind of honest man who milks his neighbor's cow through a crack in the fence, and justifies himself by claiming he owns the crack. Is this the same Saunders who went into bankruptcy to leave his trusting friends and creditors in the lurch, while he lived in luxury at an expensive hotel, and was not able to get his full discharge in bankruptcy because of fraud?*

Now the pace of the attack quickened. Saunders used racial stereotypes in several ads to attack his opponents. Crump allowed African Americans to vote in Memphis elections; this was rare in the Deep South before the Voting Rights Act of 1965. The assumption was that they would vote for candidates that Crump supported. Saunders saved his most fulsome rhetoric for Election Day: "Show to the world today that the white man and white women of Shelby County will not stand for Negroes to be called to the polls in a Democratic primary—show your white blood of resentment at this insult to your race."

Crump's organization worked hard to produce a large vote count for McAlister. Not even a last-minute court injunction by Saunders failed to prohibit McAlister from gaining thousands of votes. Horton poll watchers were beaten and driven away from the precincts. Some were arrested. The *Commercial Appeal* reporters and photographers were also mistreated, their cameras destroyed by city policemen. Nationwide press reported accounts of election violence, vote padding, illegal voting and convicted bootleggers operating voting booths. The race was so close that Horton was not declared a winner for several days afterward, with just enough rural citizens having voted to defeat McAlister and the city machine.

Saunders accepted racial prejudice and segregation, as did most people at the time. But strident, ugly anti-black statements were an aberration for him. He never again used such statements publicly, nor did he use racial caricatures, so common then, in his other advertisements. Saunders was also a reader of Thomas Paine and of his fellow Virginian, Thomas Jefferson. The same man who could use racial prejudice to his advantage was also disturbed by religious intolerance. He spoke against this intolerance during the 1928 presidential election campaign.

New York governor Al Smith was the Democratic candidate for president in 1928. Smith was an Irish Catholic son of immigrants. His character, reflected in his theme song "The Sidewalks of New York," was anathema to many non-Catholic, small-town Americans. Doubt was raised by those who called themselves patriots whether a Catholic was qualified to be president of the United States. Saunders supported his party's choice. He wrote, "Smith the Catholic! Shall we damn him because he is? Religious freedom; that was the cornerstone upon which this nation was founded." He challenged people who thought themselves better than Governor Smith. "If you haven't got the strength within yourself to forget your prejudices then pray to God to help you."

Saunders devoted most of his energy that year to finding new investors for his Sole Owner chain stores. In late October, he completed financing the Clarence Saunders Stores, Inc. The new company assumed ownership of all the stores operated by the older Clarence Saunders Corporation. The original Saunders Corporation was to remain a holding company and collector of royalty payments from franchise operators.

Two New York investment banking firms, Bertles, Rawls and Donaldson and Mitchell, Hutchins, invested $2 million in the Saunders Stores, Inc. The company issued 200,000 shares of preferred stock at $50 a share, 200,000 shares of Class A common stock and 500,000 shares of Class B common stock. The preferred stock was set to earn 7½ percent on dividends. The Class A was traded on the Exchange markets and was to earn $3 a share in dividends more than Class B. The latter stock was privately held by Saunders, Fergus Reed and William Bertles, two of the members of the principal underwriting firm. Fergus Reed was also associated with a cotton processing firm, Memphis Compress Company. The board of directors of the Clarence Saunders Stores, Inc., was said to have a net worth of $300 million. Among them was Joseph Day, one of the largest owners of Manhattan real estate. Saunders was the only Memphian on the board.

These men were of the same class who had opposed him five years before during the Piggly Wiggly stock market corner. They were not interested in his comeback until they noticed the sales data of the Sole Owner stores. "The dollar mark of profit has a swaying effect in changing a critic into a booster," Saunders said. It was a matter of pride for him to have "Wall Streeters" financing his business again. With one subtle difference though: they restricted Saunders from controlling his company's stock transactions on the Exchanges.

Saunders planned an ambitious expansion program for the Saunders Stores, Inc. He divided the nation into seven regional areas of expansion. The first group of investors contained stores already open in the South and Southwest, with new units planned for Kansas City and Denver. Another group was to continue opening units in Illinois, with 100 stores in the Chicago area, Ohio and Indiana by November 1929. A third group of investors in Detroit agreed to build 250 stores in Michigan, Ohio and Canada. Each year, the Clarence Saunders Stores, Inc., was to open stores in a new territory.

The new investment in Clarence Saunders made some of his friends in Memphis wealthier. In 1924, they had bought stock in the Clarence Saunders Corporation for $10 a share. This corporation stock was now worth $50 to $55 a share. Some of his friends sold their stock and collected huge profits. Raynor Allen, vice-president of the Clarence Saunders Corporation, refused to sell his stock, worth in his estimation $110,000. He assumed the expansion program would increase its value even more. Saunders expected to have within ten years a chain of stores with revenue of $1 billion a year with a capital investment of $50 million.

Piggly Wiggly would no longer remain an independent chain of grocery stores. The Piggly Wiggly stockholders, five years after forcing Saunders out, sold two-thirds of the controlling interest in the corporation, including all patent and licensing rights, to Kroger Grocery Company of Cincinnati, Ohio. Kroger would decide that Piggly Wiggly had too many unprofitable stores with a chaotic system of licensing franchisees and shut down a number of stores. Various pieces of the Piggly Wiggly chain were sold by their franchise owners. In October 1928, the businessmen who would create Safeway bought the Piggly Wiggly stores of Northern California and Hawaii. Andrew Williams, who helped Saunders open the first Piggly Wiggly and then operated this franchise, retired from the business a millionaire and tended to his ranch. (At a testimonial dinner, Joseph Fly spoke warmly of their shared youth at the Bowers Stores.

No mention was made of Williams's other former employer.) Another of Saunders's former associates at Piggly Wiggly made a significant income selling his franchise in the business. Stratton had earlier in the year returned to Piggly Wiggly by purchasing the fifty-seven stores in the Memphis district. Stratton operated the Memphis stores with a profit, although the year before the stores had lost money. He sold the stores within six months to Kroger, netting Stratton and his investors a $1 million gain. In another twist to the story, Kroger purchased the old Mr. Bowers chain from the Fly and Hobson Company on November 3, 1928.

If Saunders paid any attention to the dismantling of his former company, he did not speak publicly. Instead, he was busy fulfilling another of his dreams: to build an estate equal to the one he had lost four years earlier. He purchased three hundred acres of woods and pasture ten miles east of the city near the village of Germantown. He designed it to be a self-sufficient playground. He constructed an eighteen-hole golf course, tennis courts, riding paths and a landing strip for his airplanes. With a deep well and a pumping station, he filled a seventeen-acre lake. In his

The house was equipped to his inventive tastes. The bedroom closets had a light switch in the doorway. When closet doors opened, lights turned on automatically. *Courtesy of the Memphis Room, Memphis Public Library and Information Center.*

woods, he created babbling brooks and waterfalls. The water was made purified by a stone aquifer and flowed to an outdoor swimming pool. Keeping with the rural character of the estate, he named it Woodlands.

His wife and children would not live with him at Woodlands. Carolyn Saunders filed for divorce on September 27, 1928, the eve of their twenty-fifth wedding anniversary. Their marriage had become increasingly difficult through the years. In moments of stress, he had made "abusive, cutting remarks" to her, often for trivial reasons. Gradually, Saunders made her so nervous she feared for her health. His temper had grown worse because of the indictments two years before. In June, she asked him about mutual friends he had visited the previous night. He exploded into a rage. He did not "care to be questioned as to who he liked or disliked." He was "tired of being married to her and was going to put an end to it," he said.

Saunders did not contest the divorce. He did not hire a lawyer for himself and allowed Kit Williams to represent her. He expedited settlement, granting Carolyn a generous property agreement including the Goodwyn home, which he later bought back from her for $75,000. In court, she was visibly upset. She fainted once during trial testimony. Lee and Clay Saunders testified that reconciliation was impossible for their parents. Saunders never hit their mother, they testified, but he was "cold and indifferent to her, and finally his temper made her life unbearable."

Little is left to public knowledge about Mrs. Carolyn Saunders. She preferred a quiet life devoted to her children. She lived in the family home until after her daughter, Amy Clare, married some years later. Then she moved back to McLeansboro, Illinois, or she occasionally lived with her daughter and son-in-law. She kept her thoughts about her famous ex-husband private. According to her family, she never stopped loving him. And it was quite a while before she recovered from the trauma.

Saunders spent little time in Memphis during the divorce proceedings. He continued to visit his New York and Chicago investors. In December, he completed a deal that organized the Clarence Saunders Pacific Stores, with $1,500,000 capital and a stock issue. The company planned five hundred stores in California, Oregon and Washington.

While in Chicago, Saunders surprised many people again. He married Patricia Houston Bamberg on December 20, 1928. She was a twenty-nine-year-old daughter of a Tunica, Mississippi planter family. Patricia

Bamberg had separated from her first husband and moved with her son to Memphis several months before. She found a job selling life insurance for Frank Hays. An associate of her employer was Cliff Blackburn. She was an assertive woman, earning praise from Blackburn and Hays for her salesmanship despite a lack of experience. One of the customers who had bought several large policies was Clarence Saunders. Saunders eventually purchased life insurance from her worth over $2 million. He was called the most insured man in Tennessee.

Within a week of Saunders's divorce from Carolyn Saunders, Patricia Bamberg obtained her divorce. Her son, John "Tunkie," was given the surname Saunders. Together Clarence and Patricia found some happiness in her artistic talents and interests. He gave money to the Little Theater established inside the Pink Palace where Saunders had once laid out his swimming pool. Patricia Saunders discovered that her husband was an unusual philanthropist. He challenged the board to a coin toss—heads, he would pay the entire amount; tails, they would pay half. He won. His extraordinary temper did not make him a detached, calm art critic. He slashed a portrait of himself with a knife and threw the artist out of his house after paying the man his $10,000 fee.

Saunders was irritated by the gossip and rumors about him, particularly about how long and intimately he had known his second wife before their marriage. It was also obvious his children were cold to their father's new marriage. So were certain members of Memphis society, who never quite accepted Mrs. Pat Saunders as one of their own. They considered Carolyn Saunders a martyr. "Numerous other tales," he said, "that have circulated about town concerning supposively [sic] personal happenings of mine is each one a lie."

There were other, more pleasant diversions for the Sole Owner man. Early Maxwell, a sportswriter for the Commercial Appeal and a promoter, ran a professional football team. Maxwell operated on a small budget, playing at Hodges Field, a high school football stadium, before a few hundred fans. He hired former high school and local college football stars. Football now was a sideline for them, a way to make an extra seventy-five dollars on the weekend playing a young man's game.

Professional football was a new, unprofitable venture relegated to the back pages of the newspaper sports section until 1925. That year Red Grange, halfback for the University of Illinois and one of the legends of the game, signed a professional contract worth approximately $100,000, including advertising endorsements, before his academic career was complete. Grange, with his new team, the Chicago Bears of the National Football League, barnstormed the country. They played before thousands of curious fans, the largest crowds ever to see the game. Sports promoters were intrigued. If many ex-college stars like Grange could be enticed to play professional football, then sports fans would pay to watch them year after year. In 1928, Maxwell sold Saunders on the potential box office draw of this new sport.

Saunders naturally renamed the team after himself, the Clarence Saunders Sole Owner Tigers. Owning the sports team excited his promotional instincts. He used his grocery ads to promote the team. Of course, the team's attention among sports fans helped promote his Sole Owner Stores. There were always newspapermen around him at the games or practices.

Saunders enjoyed in football the competition and the sports play denied him in his youth. He was strong and athletic even in his middle

This game against the Oklahoma Indians was probably the one where Saunders had the officials start over. *Courtesy of Special Collections, McWherter Library, University of Memphis.*

years. Saunders entertained his friends with his physical prowess. He would lie on the ground face-down with arms and legs fully extended. Using just his fingertips, he would lift his entire body off the ground, a feat few could replicate. Saunders went to football practice whenever possible. Once he had the team practice at Woodlands. Their football cleats ruined the surface of his tennis courts. One player remembered Saunders at football practice: "He was out there with the team, catching punts in his three hundred dollar suits." Saunders named the starting players and designed special plays for the games, even though the Tigers had a coach whose job was to do that.

Saunders spared no expense to bring the best football teams to Memphis in the 1929 season. He paid top salaries to ex-college stars. Early in the season, he paid good teams from Oklahoma, Louisville and the Notre Dame All Stars to play the Tigers. Near the Thanksgiving holiday, he invited the Chicago Bears to play his Memphis Tigers, with all expenses paid. Red Grange made several promotional appearances in Memphis with Saunders. The Bears defeated the Tigers 39–19. They were charitable in victory, saying Saunders's team was good enough for their league. Years later, Red Grange remembered the Memphis game, and Saunders, above all others he played.

Saunders's efforts succeeded better than he had planned. Ten thousand people now crowded into Hodges Field, which could seat only fifteen hundred, to see the games. There was not enough stadium parking or ticket takers to handle the spectators. Saunders himself was late arriving to the games. On at least one occasion while the game was in progress, he rushed on the field with Maxwell toward the officials. He ordered the officials to start the game over. He and other fans had missed the kickoff, and he wanted everyone to see the whole game. The officials refused. Starting a game over was not in the rules of football. Clarence Saunders ended the argument. "I paid for the game and I am the rules of this game." The officials started the game again.

The Green Bay Packers were the best team in the National Football League that year. On the eve of their championship game, Saunders asked their player-coach, Curley Lambeau, if they would like to play one more game in Memphis. He guaranteed Lambeau a percentage of the gate and $500 per player. Lambeau agreed. Saunders called in professional players around the country to improve his team.

The Packers came to Memphis on December 16 expecting an easy game after their victory in the title game. A Milwaukee sportswriter wrote that the Packers did not finish their victory party until the train reached Memphis. They were embarrassed by the new Tigers, 20–6. They suffered in the unseasonably warm and humid weather. Lambeau was not appreciative of Saunders's arrangements. "Your officials won the game for you," he bellowed at Maxwell, who replied, "I didn't see them carry the ball for us."

Saunders called his team the "world's champions" of professional football. He enticed the Bears to a rematch game in Memphis on December 23. Despite frigid temperatures and snow covering the field, an estimated four thousand people cheered the Tigers. The Tigers won this game 16–6. The only mishap in this triumph involved his son, Lee Saunders, who played briefly but suffered a broken leg.

The Tigers had proven to him that professional football was a great success. An entire city could rally around his players, and himself. They had made this team "their own." The Tigers had become, briefly, a symbol of the city. Saunders promised football fans in Memphis that the next season was to be even better. He dreamed of sixty thousand fans cheering their Memphis Tigers against the best football players every year. He dreamed of a new stadium for his team and even selected the property to build it on. There was speculation Saunders would join the National Football League in 1930, but he decided to remain an independent team. The National Football League required its teams to play at least half of their games away from home. Saunders wanted his team to play every game in his own football stadium.

Chapter 10
BANKRUPTCY

I may be down, but I am never out.

The stock market crash of October 1929 engineered an economic collapse that changed Saunders's priorities. Frank Robertson, a bankruptcy lawyer familiar with Saunders, surmised why businessmen often fall prey to bankruptcy. While he suggested many reasons, one of his homespun proverbs was an especially accurate description of Saunders's predicament: "When times are good everybody gets big ideas and expands. And then comes a slump—and lots of us are caught with no reserves to tide us over." At Christmas, Saunders asked his bankers for a cash advance. They turned him down.

Saunders gamely tried to say that the October 1929 crash of the stock market was, on the contrary, a benefit to him. Market operators ran the Saunders Stores, Inc., stock up from twenty to fifty dollars and then seventy dollars a share during the 1929 bull market. After the crash, the speculators were reduced to unloading the shares at ten dollars. Saunders bought many of the shares at the low prices and so increased his holdings of the stock. It was those speculators who lost on the deals, not he.

Unfortunately, the first installment of the $500,000 loans for his Sole Owner expansion was due in July 1930. Bertles, Rawls and Donaldson were in no mood to relax their demands. Saunders persisted. It was urgent they provide him with more money. On three occasions he mortgaged his ex-wife's home to raise money. They offered him a deal. The Safeway chain, he was told, wanted to buy the Saunders Pacific Stores chain with an added provision he retire from the business for five years. Saunders declined their offer.

Somehow, he had to find a source of money independent of the eastern capitalists. By May, he believed he had a solution. He proposed to sell the Sole Owner stores to individuals through the issue of new stock organized by each state. New corporations were to have a representation of the whole community on each board, including women, an unusual decision then. "Who knows best about food," he explained. These state companies were to first buy existing Sole Owner stores, warehouses and equipment from the Saunders Stores, Inc. Saunders intended to maintain an active advisory role through his Clarence Saunders Corporation, collecting royalties and inspecting the operations of each store. He promised to bring more efficient distribution to the state store using truck transportation.

Saunders never had a chance to implement his state corporations plan. The Saunders Stores, Inc., had problems with local creditors. Three wholesale jobbers, whose debts totaled less than $6,000, filed a complaint in bankruptcy court on July 14. The Saunders Stores, Inc., had not paid debts owed to them, though another creditor had been paid $2,500. A preferential payment of debt to one creditor was considered an act of bankruptcy. Lovick Miles and Kit Williams filed an involuntary bankruptcy petition for the Saunders Stores, Inc., the next day, July 15. Saunders reluctantly admitted his company was insolvent. He had to file for bankruptcy on that day, for the first loan payment to the eastern banking syndicate was due on July 16 and he did not want the eastern bankers to move against him. He was sure the big creditors would seize his company's assets and "leave the little creditors holding the bag."

Judge Harry Anderson decided to appoint a receiver quickly so that the 153 Sole Owner stores in this chain would remain open. The company was not destitute, according to Saunders, who estimated that it had a cash reserve of $125,000, enough for a good manager to operate the business. Saunders wanted Leslie Stratton appointed receiver.

Stratton intended to operate the stores until the business could profitably pay its debts. He then hoped to give back the Sole Owner stores to Saunders and his stockholders and step aside. Saunders in turn had faith in his former partner's ability to turn a profit with the stores.

The chain had obligations of $1,300,000. Stratton estimated the assets of the chain at $850,000 in cash and merchandise and $900,000 in fixtures. The value of the fixtures and merchandise was tentative, depending on the stores remaining in operation. If the bankruptcy court had to sell the closed stores at auction, their value would fall. Thus the need, Stratton said, to keep the chain of stores open.

As for his own fortunes, Clarence Saunders was glum. He was not entirely broke, for his Clarence Saunders Corporation still received royalty payments from the franchise stores and even from the 153 stores now in bankruptcy. Yet it appeared he would be forced to sell his estate and move to California.

The Clarence Saunders Pacific Stores were still intact. News of the bankruptcy sparked a creditors' run on the Pacific Stores. Somehow Saunders found the cash to pay them. He was also busy that day with callers offering condolences or wanting information. Telegraph messages were stacked high on his desk. Jay Paul, a reporter for the *Commercial Appeal*, called upon him that evening. He found that Clarence Saunders had already recovered his enthusiasm. "How do you feel?" Saunders was asked:

> *Great! I've got that old time pep back. I've got this whole thing off my system. I'm ready to fight like I have never fought before. We'll make the Pacific Coast chain of stores the finest in America. Those boys on Wall Street haven't seen anything yet. My whole business career has been a huge scrap. First I broke a boycott against the W.C. Early Co. way back in 1908. Since then it has been first one thing then another. Each time I have come out of the battle a little wiser, a little stronger, and a little better prepared for the job ahead. I have only started to fight. I have simply cut another notch in my gun and I am looking for more battles to fight.*

The next day, July 16, lawyers for Bertles, Rawls and Donaldson arrived in Memphis. They opposed the bankruptcy maneuver. They asked the court not to appoint a receiver, for placing the company in the hands of a receiver protected it from all creditors. They considered themselves the preferential creditors, because Saunders had personally guaranteed the $500,000 loans for his Saunders Stores, Inc. By claiming bankruptcy for his company, he now was protected from that loan. They were suspicious of him, believing he had conspired with the local creditors to claim bankruptcy. They wondered how he could put the company in receivership without his board of directors objecting. The bankers, so they understood, had their representatives on the board.

Miles and Williams countered that Saunders had proper authority from the board—the true board of directors of the Saunders Stores, Inc. Saunders had bought so many shares after the stock market crash that he was able to call for a new election of company directors six weeks before the decision. His loyal friends and his son, Lee, were elected to the board, replacing the unsuspecting bankers. The new directors, of course, approved of everything Saunders wanted. The eastern syndicate was stunned. There was nothing they could do to prevent the appointment of Leslie Stratton as receiver except threaten legal action against Clarence Saunders.

"I may be down," Saunders gloated, "but I am never out." He promised he would make another fortune. If he could not regain his present chain, then he would make millions with a new chain of stores. He promised to keep the Sole Owner Tigers and build his new football stadium. "The stadium will have skull and crossbones for my enemies who I have slain." His followers were pleased. One shopper at a Sole Owner store said, "He may be in a tight place, but it won't be long before he has another fortune…He has plenty of nerve and is a long way from being licked."

Judge Anderson appointed a co-receiver for Sole Owner stores, apparently to placate the eastern bankers. He was J.R. Peters, a New Yorker. Peters was, in 1928, the general manager of the Piggly Wiggly Corporation and a member of Stratton's board of directors of the Memphis Piggly Wiggly Stores until Kroger bought both companies. He became a consultant for chain stores in financial difficulty.

During the first week of August, Saunders had a change of heart about California. The eastern syndicate lured him to New York promising a compromise plan to reorganize the finances of the Saunders Stores, Inc. Saunders arrived with Peters, who acted as an intermediary. The bankers surprised Saunders with a court summons for their lawsuit against him. Saunders, furious at their trickery, had to be restrained by Peters, who was able to get Saunders out of town, safely dodging the summons.

Peters negotiated a compromise between the bankers and Saunders in August. He convinced Saunders to assume, with his personal wealth and with the Clarence Saunders Corporation, the debts of the Saunders

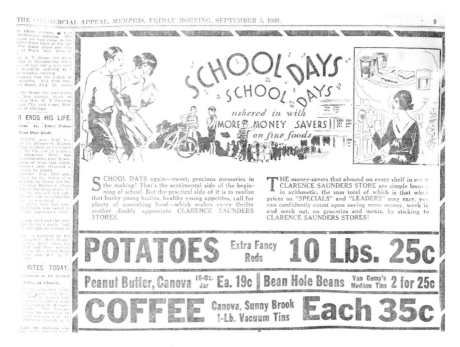

The idyllic scene of this advertisement, dated September 5, was a contrast to the frazzled state of Saunders's mind and the financial health of the Clarence Saunders Stores. *Courtesy of Special Collections, McWherter Library, University of Memphis.*

Stores, Inc., due the bankers. The bankers, in turn, agreed not to prosecute a suit against Saunders. Both parties agreed to the reorganization plan. In effect the bankers, Saunders and other investors were to put more cash into the business and purchase debenture bonds of three- to five-year maturation. The bonds were to help pay the debts of the Saunders Stores, Inc. In return, the parties involved received more shares of common and preferred stock. For the plan to succeed, the chain of stores had to make a profit again.

In October, Stratton reported that the Sole Owner stores were in stable financial shape, considering the poor economic circumstances. He expected to show a small profit despite a decline in sales volume and in merchandise prices. He achieved these positive results by drastically cutting expenses. Stratton and Peters together asked Judge Anderson to continue their tenure as receivers. The business depression concerned Stratton. Closing the stores, he reminded the court, would put one thousand people out of work.

The Wyatt family of Dallas was not satisfied with the management of the Saunders Stores, Inc., estate. The company still owed $111,000 more than its assets. They demanded that Judge Anderson dissolve the receivership and sell the stores at auction. They were convinced that was the only sure method left to secure any of their debt. They also insisted the assets of the Sole Owner were over-valued, especially the trademark rights to the name of Clarence Saunders. On the other hand, the eastern bankers supported Stratton and Peters's efforts. Judge Anderson postponed any decision on the receivership until January 1931. The two receivers continued to negotiate with all the creditors. By December 23, they had persuaded every creditor to accept the reorganization plan. Peters, as a show of good faith in the plan, invested $25,000.

Saunders continued to suffer from his own embarrassing financial problems. Less than two years before, Saunders had been fêted in California for opening forty-six new Sole Owner stores in one day. Admiration had now turned to suspicion. The State of California Corporation Department suspended his stock sale license on February 17, 1931. They claimed he sold stock of two new companies, the Clarence Saunders Northern California and the Southern California Stores, on the pretense of expanding the two chains. Instead, the department charged, he diverted $40,000 from Northern California to his Clarence Saunders Corporation in Memphis. They accused him of paying his family and friends from the California companies rather than from the cash-short Tennessee company and of charging country club dues and other extravagant living expenses to the companies.

The Corporation Department in April expressed these complaints in a formal hearing. B.A. Reiland, once a secretary for Saunders's Northern California Company, and other disgruntled employees were the state's witnesses against Saunders. Reiland even testified that Saunders walked the Oakland streets selling stock certificates.

Saunders denied the charges brought against him. The State of California was persecuting him, just as "the wolves of Wall Street" had persecuted him before. "I thought California wanted outsiders," he said. Saunders reminded the department he had brought investment into the state. He insisted the $40,000 in question was a legitimate royalty payment to his Clarence Saunders Corporation. He insisted the payment to his friends and family was for work performed in the state.

The hearings were most unpleasant for him. He felt his reputation was at stake. Saunders lost control while on the witness stand. His own attorney demanded he close his mouth: "You're going to put your foot into it." "I'm being overruled by my own attorney!" he shouted back.

The value of his California stores was at stake. Saunders arranged to sell all of his stores in the state to the Continental Chain Stores for $1 million. He hoped the sale would end his business interests in California, but the sale dissolved. The same week, creditors of the Southern California Stores placed that chain under bankruptcy. Saunders assumed that he would not receive any money from the eventual sale of those stores.

In Memphis, the reorganization plan for the Saunders Stores, Inc., also failed. Judge Anderson ordered the receivership dissolved and the chain sold at auction as eleven separate units of stores. The proceeds of the auction were to satisfy, in part, the debt owed to the creditors. On April 6, the twenty-six stores in the Memphis unit were sold for $100,000, well under their assessed value. The entire Saunders Stores chain was sold for only $376,100. The buyer for the Memphis stores was P.H. Verner, a Memphis warehouseman who was a proxy for Stratton. Judge Anderson was disappointed in the results of the sale. He ordered the auction to cease until new bids were submitted. One week later, the Kroger Company's bid of $130,500 for the Memphis stores was accepted. Kroger planned to keep only ten of the Sole Owner stores open in Memphis under their trademark name. Leslie Stratton had failed in his bid to purchase all of the Memphis stores. But Stratton, determined to operate another chain of stores for his own profit, acquired some of the leases to the vacant Sole Owner Stores.

The receivers, trustees and their attorneys together demanded fees of nearly $200,000 to be paid from the money raised by the auction. Stratton asked for $53,000 and Peters demanded $40,000. Lovick Miles and Kit Williams, their attorneys, submitted $12,500 each as the proper fee for their services. The creditors were furious with these demands. They, led again by the Wyatt family, filed a protest in the bankruptcy court. If those fees were awarded, the creditors would have only approximately $100,000 to divide among them. As the combined debt of the Saunders Stores, Inc., was $1,400,000, the creditors were to receive as repayment less than ten cents upon the dollar.

Saunders spoke out in favor of the creditors. Stratton and Peters performed a "great job," he said with sarcasm. He had entrusted them with a business that at the time still held a cash surplus. Within a year, the business lost more than $200,000 and then closed. They failed in their official duty: to protect the creditors from loss. Yet they still demanded large fees for their services. It appeared to Saunders that they had taken advantage of his chain's financial problems to enrich themselves. Stratton, stung by Saunders criticism, said he managed the chain with better judgment than Saunders had before him. He made no apology for the large fee demand. The creditors, he pointed out, had approved the reorganization plan. It was unfortunate the plan failed and the chain could not be salvaged from bankruptcy.

Bankruptcy referee John Walker ruled in favor of the creditors. He cut Stratton's fee to $13,000 and Peters's fee to $10,000. Miles and Williams received only $250 each. They immediately filed an appeal to Judge Anderson. Walker awarded the money saved from the fees to the creditors.

The foreclosure of the Saunders Stores, Inc., and then the California chains had its toll on the parent company, the Clarence Saunders Corporation. The corporation had lost its income from royalties. Only about one hundred Sole Owner Stores remained in operation, all owned by independent franchisees. Their royalty payments ceased when the corporation had stopped offering purchase services for them. The corporation's stock, once valued at $110 a share, or $1,500,000, was now considered worthless.

Saunders filed a voluntary petition of bankruptcy for himself and his corporation on June 16, 1931. He listed assets of $287,105 and debts of $402,000. He turned over to bankruptcy referee C.L. King nearly all his possessions, even his watch. He assumed he would lose his life insurance policies, Carolyn Saunders's Goodwyn Avenue home and the Woodlands property. Saunders reflected on his misfortune. He had spent almost $500,000 on the Woodlands estate. Now it was appraised at $200,000. The bankruptcy officials would probably sell it for less. The Internal Revenue Service intended to collect from the bankrupt corporation $63,000 income taxes due. Trustee Frank Robertson was appointed to oversee the estate on June 30. On the same day, the California Corporation Department revoked forever his privileges to sell stock of the Clarence Saunders companies in the state.

It was not certain if the bankruptcy action would deprive Saunders of the business rights to his own name. He said, "I feel like a new born baby without a name." He was not daunted. Twice before he had created fortunes of at least $3 million within three years; he vowed to do it again, only this time he promised to earn his fortune in two years and seven months. He would build the most elaborate, most astounding retail store. He needed $50,000 to begin the project. Saunders expected no difficulty finding investors. People were always willing to back him, and his backers had always profited from their investment.

Three months later, Saunders had already found his backers. On October 14, his full-page advertisement announced the brand-new Clarence Saunders Sole Owner Store. In the ad, he portrayed his confident spirit as a cat scratching his enemies.

Saunders and his construction crew remodeled the Winkleman Bakery at North Main and Jefferson for his new store. The building was three stories, giving Saunders a much larger retail space than any of his earlier stores.

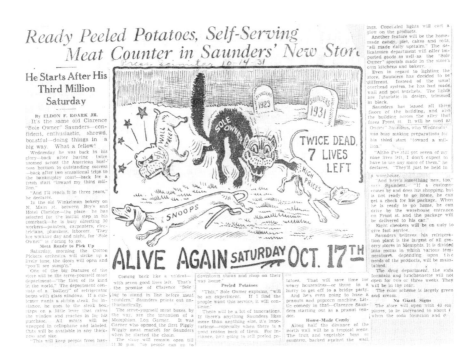

Saunders, the wildcat, had lost two of his "nine lives." Saunders was asked if this was the best time to open a business. "Yes, this is the best time in the world. That is, for me." *Courtesy of the Memphis Room, Memphis Public Library and Information Room.*

The phrase "supermarket" was used to describe grocery stores with self-service for at least 75 percent of the grocery items but clerk service for special items. Saunders offered many amenities, like this bakery, in his new supermarket. *Courtesy of the Memphis Room, Memphis Public Library and Information Center.*

On October 17, hundreds of shoppers waited in line to enter the new store while the Cotton Pickers Band played "Happy Days Are Here Again." Saunders ran out of shopping baskets for his many customers. The grand opening was broadcast on radio. Saunders mounted the orchestra platform to speak: "I know many of you came out of curiosity…I am curious too. Curious to see how long I could keep going broke and still keep coming back."

The Great Depression continued to inflict hardship. An estimated one-third of the workforce was unemployed by the end of 1932. Under these circumstances, Saunders felt compelled to lower the profit margin of some grocery commodities. In April 1932, he dropped the price of a quart of milk to seven cents and a pint to four cents. This price was at least two cents cheaper than what dairymen charged for milk delivered to the home. One dairy charged Saunders and the Shelby County Milk

This is the grand opening of his new store at 93 North Main. It was the size of a department store. Saunders added a new innovation, packages of meat individually wrapped in cellophane, displayed in open refrigerators. *Courtesy of the Memphis Room, Memphis Public Library and Information Center.*

Producers Association with a conspiracy to drive down milk prices and that Saunders had a financial interest in the association. Saunders replied that their accusations were not true; he had no agreements with the association. He priced his milk to earn for his business only one cent per quart.

He boldly announced his new expansion of the Sole Owner Stores. He had leased property in the suburban Crosstown neighborhood. A billboard marked the location. On this billboard was the caricature of a "very impish imp" prancing over a grave. Adjacent to the imp was his message: "Here's my graveyard. Clarence Saunders is the ghost that will walk here a long time, rattling the bones to the tune of cheaper and cheaper prices."

On that spot Saunders promised to build a store larger and grander than his present Sole Owner Store. He called it his "mammoth store."

This is the drawing of his proposed "mammoth store"; it was to have sixty thousand square feet of space in a two-story building with twenty check stands. Saunders wanted to sell auto supplies, drugs, cosmetics and similar items. *Courtesy of the Memphis Room, Memphis Public Library and Information Center.*

Saunders expected to raise $100,000 to build the store. Excavation work began in the first week of March 1932. Amy Clare Saunders struck the ceremonial first spade of dirt on the construction site for her father. Within weeks after construction began, contractors stopped work on the mammoth store because they had not been paid. They left the bare foundation in place. The store was never completed, and for years the foundation lay undisturbed. People called it "Saunders's basement."

Bankruptcy difficulties continued to plague Saunders. He was sued by Charles G. Smith on May 19, 1932, for debts owed on the Woodlands estate. Smith had originally sold the estate land to Saunders in 1928. He purchased the estate at the bankruptcy auction for $92,000. In July, M.C. Brock sued to collect on a $10,000 note Saunders had signed. Saunders placed as collateral his furnishings and other possessions at the Woodlands estate. Saunders was ordered not to sell this property but to turn it over to Brock. Then the Saunders family moved out of Woodlands. Smith, on July 23, opened Woodlands to the public as a recreation park. In 1932, Patricia Saunders had given birth to their daughter, Ann, in that home. He promised to earn back the Woodlands estate and rename it for her someday.

Saunders was ready to expand his Sole Owner business again. He rented an abandoned post office building on Union Avenue, a busy thoroughfare connecting the city with its eastern suburbs. The new store had twelve thousand square feet, twice the space of his North Main store. It was large enough for his bakery, with revolving ovens, his soda fountain and meat department. Saunders no longer expressed a desire for a chain of many small stores. The large store on Union was equal in size to twenty-five of his first Piggly Wigglys. He was not ready, though, to start work again on the unfinished Crosstown store until later in the year.

President Franklin Delano Roosevelt took the oath of office on March 4, 1933. There was a sense of emergency when Roosevelt assumed his responsibilities. He promised American citizens a "New Deal," a cheerful, confident fight against the Depression. Clarence Saunders, supporting Roosevelt's new mood of optimism, gave to his employees a 10 percent pay raise in late March 1933. They were not surprised by Saunders's generous actions. One employee said, "Most of us had been with him for a long time. We stuck to him in the lean years, and now he's coming through for us now that conditions are better."

The National Recovery Act imposed the first minimum wage and maximum hour laws for the nation. Saunders no longer had the investment to pay the extra wages cost imposed on him by the NRA. Apparently he tried to persuade his employees to accept management status, which was not covered by the wage and hour codes. But their loyalty only stretched so far; not enough of them agreed to this concession. Within six months after the NRA was enacted, he decided to close the two Sole Owner Stores before his creditors filed for bankruptcy. Oddly, two days prior he had signed a labor agreement with the butchers, granting them a pay raise. In his last Sole Owner advertisement, he was philosophical about his most recent failure. Believing Roosevelt was trying to do the right thing, Saunders supported the NRA in principle. Someday, he reasoned, the NRA would help other businesses prosper, even though his stores did not. "It was," he said, "like the fortunes of war, some die so that others may live."

As fate would have it, the creditors of his bankrupt Clarence Saunders Corporation received the last of its assets the same week he closed the stores. Charles Bryan, attorney for trustee Frank Robertson, collected $38,000 from the many life insurance policies Saunders lost to the trustee. Most of the money was used to satisfy an income tax bill of Saunders's.

Chapter 11
ROBOT GROCERY STORE

I expect Keedoozle to dazzle them.

Saunders did not tolerate his business failure. The economic depression was a depression of his spirit as well. He became more erratic and unsure of what to do. In 1934, he promoted a cleaning product called "Evernew." It was supposed to clean laundry, but some customers charged in court that the product ruined clothing. That same year, he became a victim of a con artist. A man purporting to be a former German naval officer and spy convinced Saunders that he had buried treasure on the island of Haiti. He only needed a few thousand dollars to retrieve the treasure. The con man traveled as far as New Orleans before Saunders realized he had been fooled. The perpetrator was arrested and brought back to Memphis for trial. Many people laughed at Saunders during this episode. The swindler's overbearing behavior in court and his odd stories were the fodder for many jokes.

Somehow Saunders had found a new challenge in the business he still loved. In his first stores, frugal management and few employees created a great success. But he created the second stores with far more employees and had less success. What he needed, in this poor economy, was a store that required few employees again. New technology could do the work that humans once did. Vending machines, some powered by electricity, dispensed candy bars, chewing gum and bottles of soda. Customers deposited coins into a slot that activated the machines to release the products. The Automats in New York and Philadelphia offered plates of food behind a glass door. Customers deposited coins to open a glass door and retrieve the food.

Why not use this electrical and mechanical technology to sell groceries in a supermarket? Lee Saunders and his father were avid ham radio hobbyists. Their interest in this technology led to their friendship with Victor Laughter, a self-taught electrical engineer, whom they respected as a genius. In 1912, when he was twenty-four, Laughter engineered the first wireless radio broadcast in Memphis. During World War I, he served on the front lines, monitoring radio transmissions for the Signal Corps. By 1931, he held eighteen patents for radio and electronic innovations.

With Laughter's expertise, Saunders could stock groceries in metal chutes like a vending machine. His customers would enter the store and notice glass display cases with a sample item of a product behind each case, like the Automat. Beside each display item was a slot. Instead of

The next five photos, undated, were created inside a working store and are arranged to show how it operated. Saunders is standing to the left watching the line of people waiting. His employees gave the customer in line a "key." *Courtesy of the Memphis Room, Memphis Public Library and Information Center.*

An unidentified man is describing the key to a large crowd. The "key" was a fiber rod, approximately nine inches long that looked "like a red ball on a stick." At first, the store had only twenty-four keys. *Courtesy of the Memphis Room, Memphis Public Library and Information Center.*

The shoppers put their key into the slot next to the display item. The red light flashed inside the bulb when the key made electrical contact. The items were stored in chutes above the display area. *Courtesy of the Memphis Room, Memphis Public Library and Information Center.*

Left: When the key is inserted into the slot, electrical contact is made with the particular chute. The cashier inserted the shopper's key into the master keyhole, which released the items from the chutes, as seen here. *Courtesy of the Memphis Room, Memphis Public Library and Information Center.*

Below: The conveyor belt moved the items down to the cashier's desk. The shopper at the counter and two Keedoozle employees are finishing the transaction. At the far left corner of the room, Saunders and three other employees watch. *Courtesy of the Memphis Room, Memphis Public Library and Information Center.*

using coins to start the transaction, Saunders would give his customers a key. When they inserted the key into a slot, electric signals would activate. But the grocery items would be released all at once, not one at a time. At the cashier's desk, his employee would insert the key into a master slot. Now all the selected items would release from the chutes to a conveyor belt and then be brought to the cashier's desk.

He believed his machinery would transact sales faster than the most efficient supermarket, using fewer employees. It would require only two men to operate—one in the rear to keep stock units in the chutes filled and the other in front to release purchases and take money from customers. Automation's speed in delivering the products would make it possible for a store to handle ten times the volume of sales of a supermarket at 10 percent less business expense. Automation eliminated theft, errors and waste by employees and customers. He was convinced the new store would change the grocery business in as profound a manner as his self-service arrangement had nearly twenty years before.

And that was it. He had a name—Keedoozle. Saunders used his celebrity status to sell the Keedoozle idea to investors and the press. He described his store as an "automatic marketing device" or an "electric service store." It was assumed the name was derived from the key, as the "key does it all" in his electrical system. Often Saunders wryly said that the name meant nothing. "I just made a name up that would be different. Just like Piggly Wiggly." Memphis newspapers called it "the robot grocery store."

On November 22, 1935, Saunders chartered the Keedoozle Corporation with a capitalization of $500,000 and fifty thousand shares of stock already sold. Lee Saunders and Robert Black were his company officers. Robert Black represented a group of investors from St. Louis and Chicago.

Saunders leased retail property at 1628 Union. The storefront was small, only fifty feet wide with twelve-foot ceilings. Floor space was at a premium. He constructed the stockroom chutes on a balcony above and to the rear of the cashier's desk. At first he expected to open January 20, 1936, but that opening date was premature. On January 10, 1936, he said the Keedoozle would probably open in February.

Yet that announcement was also premature. Saunders again delayed opening the Keedoozle store. Saunders relied on few people to build his

Keedoozle. Laughter designed all the wire and solder circuits—quite a feat, for the Keedoozle store reportedly had ten thousand electrical connections. He cast all the dies and knew how to tool the machinery. A crew of about eleven electricians, machinists and helpers worked at the machine shop on Chelsea Avenue near Watkins and the store site. One man, Sam Floyd, was responsible for all the mechanical drawings, which made him indispensable to the project. Designing and assembling the intricate machinery required more time than Saunders had expected. A pattern had been set in the Keedoozle project.

In late June 1936, Saunders believed the store was ready for national publicity. *Time* magazine dispatched a correspondent to Memphis to see the "most original grocer in the United States." Saunders offered this quote: "Within a year I'll be worth $10,000,000. I won't have that much on hand but I'll be worth it because I'll have Keedoozle. In twelve months I will have stores doing a million dollars worth of business a day." Saunders made an odd impression on the correspondent and his editors. The magazine didn't quite believe Saunders would make a third fortune with the Keedoozle. But they gave credit to his remarkable optimism and printed many legendary stories of Saunders's career. They retold one story of how Saunders had in 1923 traveled to Wall Street with bags of gold to buy Piggly Wiggly stock only to lose his entire fortune. They wrote that Saunders did his best thinking in the bathtub.

Ernie Pyle, the freelance newspaper columnist, also visited Saunders in June. Saunders never expressed any regrets to Pyle. The writer asked him about the bankruptcies and lost fortunes. Everything worked out for the best, Saunders explained. If he had not lost his chain of conventional stores, he would not have experimented with the Keedoozle. The new store would be his greatest accomplishment. Then Saunders indulged in his own legend building: "I didn't have a cent, not even a car. When I go down, I go to the bottom. That's how I do everything." He related to the writer how after he lost the second fortune, he immediately leased one of the most expensive apartments in the city, although he and Pat Saunders were living on her allowance.

Saunders told Pyle he had been working on this venture in his mind for three or four years. Saunders candidly admitted to him the investors from St. Louis and Chicago were not confident of the idea, "but they trust me." When Pyle learned of the Keedoozle system, he also expressed his

Newspaper columnist Ernie Pyle wrote, "Somehow you get the idea that anybody who bucks the established order in a big way and loses is a quack or a freak. That's what I supposed Saunders was. Why, he's just like anybody else." *Courtesy of the Memphis Room, Memphis Public Library and Information Center.*

doubts: "I told him it seemed a hard way to buy some groceries. But he says the point is that it's faster…a store can handle a much bigger volume than a usual store of similar size."

Delegates of the June 1936 National Association of Retail Grocers Convention learned of the Keedoozle. Rival grocers contributed at least half of the investment money in the Keedoozle. They believed Keedoozle, if it worked as well as Saunders claimed, would change the way many conventional grocers operated their businesses, as had his Piggly Wiggly. Their investment was a measure of their respect and fear of Saunders's ability. One of the first to invest in Keedoozle was the Weingarten family, owners of a department store and grocery chain in Houston, Texas. Nearly twenty years before, they had rebuilt their stores for self-service after first observing Piggly Wiggly.

Still, the Keedoozle was not ready for shoppers. Six months later, in February 1937, Saunders promised Keedoozle would open in March.

Saunders commissioned a newsreel film of the store in operation. The two-minute film was one of the first color films created in Memphis. He likely used it to show prospective investors. *Courtesy of the Memphis Room, Memphis Public Library and Information Center.*

He gave a tour of the store at 1628 Union to Memphis newspaper reporters. Saunders allowed them to pick some groceries with a key and then watch the machinery work upstairs. The *Press-Scimitar* reporter wrote, "A moving conveyor belt in the bottom, above are racks and racks of groceries, each rack lets loose one item for each time the bulb on the key flashed."

In newspaper ads, Saunders touted the advantages of machine-delivered goods and plastic packaging: "Ladies can wear evening gowns in the Keedoozle. It is as clean as a bank. They don't have to touch a thing. They can't...Foiled is the lady who punctured the skin of a ripe tomato with a rapier-like fingernail, foiled is he who would slip an extra box of pepper into his pocket; foiled is the Spoilage Ogre who eats fruit and vegetable profits."

At last, in May 1937, Saunders was ready to unveil the Keedoozle. Saunders expected a large crowd of curious visitors on the grand opening

Robot Grocery Store

In this photo, Saunders is showing a shopper how to select fresh vegetables with the key. Each produce and meat product was sliced or cubed to fit more readily into the Keedoozle chutes. *Courtesy of the Memphis Room, Memphis Public Library and Information Center.*

Shoppers crowded around the cashier's cage demanding a key, shouting, "Take my dollar!" "I'm so tired of explaining things that I can't think," Saunders said at the end of the day. *Courtesy of the Memphis Room, Memphis Public Library and Information Center.*

day. He requested that shoppers place a dollar deposit for the key during the grand opening day so those who wanted to purchase goods could do so without a lengthy wait for one of the twenty-four keys. He reminisced with his newspaper friends about his spectacular grand openings of the past. "This time," he said, "Keedoozle [grand opening] will be quiet. The electronic miracle will take the place of outside attractions. I expect Keedoozle to dazzle them."

The grand opening was anything but quiet. Many customers liked the Keedoozle. The store was clean, and when the machinery worked, their shopping was quick. Saunders's greatest attraction was the cheap prices. Some housewives with plenty of time on their hands always shopped in the Keedoozle. They waited patiently for the repair crew to finish their work. Then they bought the item at a price cheaper than they paid elsewhere in the city. Saunders kept prices low even though his labor costs soared because of the constant need for electricians.

In a perverse way, the glass display of the Keedoozle encouraged impulse buying of products one would never have thought to purchase. Paul Coppock, a reporter for the *Commercial Appeal*, was fascinated with the Keedoozle. On a visit, he purchased a box of chocolate-covered caviar that remained uneaten in his refrigerator for three years.

Saunders claimed only a 2 percent error rate for the Keedoozle system, but that was too many for him. "Errors brought headaches," he said. Saunders was confounded by problems he had not expected. Many of his customers in a grocery store frequently made their selections in a random manner. They changed their minds about a selection and picked something else, or they forgot what they had ordered. The cashier would have to sort out which grocery items on the conveyor belt the customer really wanted and then retrieve the correct items from the stockroom. At the same time, the cashier had to adjust the customer's total purchase on the adding machine. The electrical system for the individual keys was inflexible, for Saunders could not afford to activate more than twenty-four keys. Thus, only twenty-four people could logically shop at the same time in the store without confusing each other's order.

He explained, in February 1938, some of his decisions for the Keedoozle:

I had to go through the complicated mechanical system to find what worked. It cost over $200,000. We made many improvements in our electrical

Many shoppers disliked purchasing fresh meat or produce without touching their choice. Saunders installed ordinary display equipment for meat, produce and delicatessen merchandise. "Machines can't think for you," he said, "they can't explain to a customer." *Courtesy of the Memphis Room, Memphis Public Library and Information Center.*

system but as we did so costs went higher and higher. Now costs of mechanical equipment will be cut by 2/3, $5,000 compared to $15,000. The Memphis store is a demonstration point for operation of the system.

Then, Saunders introduced a new "magic key" to make the Keedoozle system more accessible to shoppers. Attached to the lip of each key was a roll of adding machine paper and an ink cylinder. The key now printed a sales slip for the shoppers with the name of the article and its price. Inside each slot by a glass display case was a line of type arranged to imprint the name of the article and the price. When customers inserted their key into the slot, the attached adding machine paper received its imprint. Customers were able to change their minds by crossing out an item on their list. His electricians also rearranged the circuitry to allow more than twenty-four keys to be used by shoppers simultaneously.

He reopened the Keedoozle store in May 1938. In his advertisement on May 18, he implored his readers who were disenchanted with the Keedoozle to try his store again. He was positive he had eliminated the mechanical problems that beset his innovation of the retail grocery store: "Habit, that miserable thing called habit has taken more people to the wrong place...So when you read this, habit will impel you to go to the familiar place yet reason and the prompting of what is good for you will tell you that Keedoozle is the place to go."

The new key failed to work. Saunders closed the Keedoozle again in late October 1938 to redesign the key mechanism. After several months of experiment, his crew manufactured a third key out of sheet metal in the shape of a pistol.

Financial problems distracted Saunders from his efforts on the Keedoozle. He had moved Patricia and Ann back to Woodlands, which

The tip of the "gun" contained the adding machine tape and ink cylinder. The customer inserted the tip into the slot and squeezed the trigger. That imprinted the name of the product, its numeral code and its price on the tape. *Courtesy of the Memphis Room, Memphis Public Library and Information Center.*

he renamed Annswood. He believed that he had an understanding for a payment schedule for the mortgage. Either the mortgage holder disagreed or Saunders had not made enough payments. Bill Terry, star player for the baseball New York Giants, bought the estate at a courthouse auction for $75,000. Saunders filed suit to block the sale. Saunders did not want to surrender the estate, insisting he was still the proper owner. But three months after filing, he dropped the suit. This was taking too much of his time away from the Keedoozle. "I've got my hands full, and my time is too valuable." He tried to conceal his disappointment with a stoic logic: "Since life is a win or lose game, one must be able to lose as well as win."

Saunders opened his Keedoozle at 1628 Union for the third time on February 25, 1939. To his newspaper ad readers, he chattered, "New Electric Baby all dressed up in blue and as beautiful as the song 'Blue Heaven.' This is the new Keedoozle and so perfect for pleasure you will

Clarence, Patricia and Ann Saunders sit for a portrait at Annswood. They moved out for the last time in the summer of 1938. Young Ann lived in the house just long enough to remember her bedroom, which was blue with silver stars. *Courtesy of the Memphis Room, Memphis Public Library and Information Center.*

think you have visited the home of the fairies. You will be joyfully thrilled to see such beauty, such order, and quickness in shopping."

"This time," he said in the ad, "without confusion or error." He talked of the hard work he and his men had expended through the years to perfect the Keedoozle. He prevailed upon his readers to value this effort and visit the store. The Keedoozle was destined to succeed, and people would travel to Memphis just to see it.

The magazine *Business Week* sent reporters to Memphis in April. They were fascinated by the Keedoozle mechanisms, which to them resembled a Rube Goldberg cartoon. Saunders's confidence and vivid style charmed them. They wrote: "Clarence Saunders at 9:00 A.M. bustled about showing novice shoppers how to use his new-type key. The cash register was playing a cheerful obbligato to the thumping of the cans as they hit the conveyor on their way to become sales…The boss was in his element."

Saunders informed the magazine that he could produce a complete store without a meat department to sell for $5,600. He said he had sold

Saunders chartered the Keedoozle Stores, Inc., in September 1939, and issued 2,000 shares of preferred stock and 200,000 shares of common stock. Jesse Norfleet, owner of this certificate, invested in Saunders's ideas from the beginning of Piggly Wiggly. *Courtesy of Special Collections, McWherter Library, University of Memphis.*

franchise rights to investors in several large cities and that he was near finishing the deal for rights in New York and the New England region. Soon he would ship Keedoozle stores to his franchisees.

Earlier, Saunders had leased a three-story building downtown at Third and Jefferson. The building contained thirty thousand square feet and, next to it, parking space for three hundred cars. Saunders spent $50,000 remodeling the building into a lavish showcase for his Keedoozle. On one floor he designed the Rose Room, a ladies' powder room staffed with a uniformed maid. On another floor he planned to build the Keedoozle machinery for his franchisees.

He closed the Union Avenue Keedoozle on October 27, 1939. Again, he said it was an experimental store that proved to him certain principles in mechanical merchandising. Now the experimental stage was past. On December 8, Saunders announced the grand opening for his new

Inside, Saunders constructed a bakery, with the ovens controlled by electric timer switches. The front wall plate glass, as in his last two Sole Owner Stores, allowed shoppers to watch the bakers make cakes, pies and bread. *Courtesy of the Memphis Room, Memphis Public Library and Information Center.*

Keedoozle the following day: "We shall kiss, we shall love, for the new Keedoozle will so startle the world that he who is dumb will speak and he who is deaf shall hear. All of you of spirit, of understanding are cordially invited to come and be one of us and the many who will celebrate by their presence this coming-out party of the Keedoozle."

As was his custom, Saunders spent a sleepless night preparing for the grand opening. The next morning, he greeted the multitude of people waiting at the store entrance, who were so numerous he was forced to limit the number of visitors inside. Saunders moved about the store accompanied by representatives of a Philadelphia grocery business, the American Stores. The *Commercial Appeal* lauded the Keedoozle, calling it "a swift and whirring mechanical marvel…humming along on its first day."

Unfortunately for Saunders, the Keedoozle was again plagued by mechanical difficulties. It was not simply the key. Cans and bottles often fell out of the chutes at inappropriate moments and were damaged. At first, these items landed on wooden trays, which caused much of the breakage. Saunders's crew replaced the trays with a cloth belt parallel to the conveyor belt. But the conveyor belts were an intractable problem that needed constant repair and maintenance. Many cans and bottles also simply rolled off the belts or crashed into more fragile items. The crew tried to avoid breakage by placing the glass bottle packages on the lowest tier of chutes. They positioned merchandise in the chutes so that a fragile item would not be crushed by a large 303 can of tomatoes. No matter what they did, the large can would break glass bottles. Whenever a glass bottle shattered, the crew would stop the machinery. Someone would clean the mess, adjust the belts or chutes, replace the products and then resume the process.

Chapter 12
MY LAST BIG PLUNGE

Back to my Keedoozle, back to the top one last time.

S aunders again endured the complaints and the jokes he had heard the previous two years about his Keedoozle. Saunders resented these comments and the laughter. Already, he had let that resentment show in his grand opening ad:

> *A Keedoozle if you please, that no one will criticize except those who have cobwebby brains and already have been told to stay away, but, of course, won't…Those who do not now acclaim will be mighty proud away from home to brag and say, oh yes, Clarence is so and so and such a good friend, maybe; not hardly speaking to me at Memphis or else I don't speak to them.*

He carried that anger home as well. A young friend of Ann's vividly remembered how his white hair contrasted so sharply with his red face during an outburst. Mr. Saunders was furious that an old acquaintance he no longer considered a friend wanted to spend an evening with the Saunderses. Three days before Christmas, he was stopped by the police for running a red light. Soon there was a fight, and the police arrested Saunders. Although he protested what he called the abuse of the officers, eventually Saunders paid the fine for drunken driving.

KEEDOOZLE

MY HALF-BROTHERS

I Guess They Are My Half-Brothers

My big bud, the super-market; my little bud, the smaller grocer, both loved me so much they copied my ways. Wasn't that sweet?

They spurned me at first. I was disowned. I had disgraced them with Self-Service. They repented. Brother Clarence, after all, has really got a good idea with Self-Service, but we don't need Brother Clarence around. Brother Clarence is too unpredictable. We like DIGNITY in the family circle.

Oh, Boy! What a shove outside did Clarence get! He wasn't in the family any more. But Self-Service was and how! The half-brothers of Clarence bragged about Self-Service. THEY did it! Brother Clarence had nothing to do with Self-Service.

Brother Clarence, cold and hungry, put his brain to work. Out comes Keedoozle. Half-brothers smirk and frown. They say, "Another crazy idea of Clarence's. It won't work." "Why did we ever have such a brother as Clarence? He's always causing trouble."

Why did I ever have such brothers? That is MY query.

Even if I am the black sheep of the family, I produce "All wool—a yard wide!"

Washington reports a decline in food prices, less than one percent. Keedoozle has beat them to the "gun" with a 10% cut.

Shut your mouth forever about food prices if you don't trade at Keedoozle. Dumb Doras are not supposed to be able to talk.

In several ads, like this one, Saunders revealed his frustrations and hurt feelings. *Courtesy of Special Collections, McWherter Library, University of Memphis.*

By this time, Ann was no longer home during the school months. Like other children of prominent families, she was sent to boarding school, hers near Philadelphia. Saunders visited as often as he could on his business trips east. With her, the frustrated businessman could put aside his weary concerns. Once, upon her dare, he ate crackers and hot sauce until his eyes watered.

The new store remained open for only one year. The investment from the American Stores had not materialized. In December 1940, Saunders closed his store at Third and Jefferson. The Internal Revenue Service seized assets from the Keedoozle Stores Incorporated and Keedoozle Corporation to pay $3,900 in taxes owed from the years 1936, 1937 and 1938. Once again, Saunders chartered a new company, the Keedoozle Automatic Company in Chicago, as if he would bounce back with another store.

But a profound tragedy devastated the Saunders family. Clay Saunders failed in nearly every endeavor he had attempted. His marriage to Julia Moore dissolved in less than four years. She filed for divorce, she said, because Clay Saunders's temper was "violent and ungovernable." Not long before, Clay had been arrested for assault after a traffic accident. Julia and the newspapers had politely not mentioned that he was dying from his alcoholism. The family would send him away for treatment only to watch him return home drinking. Clay Saunders died on August 16 at the age of thirty-one.

He was buried in his mother's town, McLeansboro. Clay left a young daughter, Kay. The Saunderses embraced Julia and her daughter Kay into the family. Clarence Saunders was a doting grandfather to his grandchildren: Kay; Barry and Linda, the children of Lee and Mary Saunders; and Carolyn Dean, the daughter of Amy Clare and Minor Dean. He read stories to them and took them to the zoo or the Indian Mounds. Grandson Barry watched the crew at the Keedoozle machine shop and store. When he became old enough, he helped his father and grandfather in their work.

Clarence Saunders assuaged his grief through his work. The United States' entry into World War II postponed his plans to reopen the Keedoozle. Metal and electrical materials were rationed for the war effort. Saunders created a new venture with the war rationing in mind. He converted a bowling alley into a large woodwork shop. Saunders manufactured toy wagons and baby strollers out of wood and a few nails. He arranged his shop production to require little machinery. He even utilized scrap wood to make broomsticks.

Two years after his son's death, Saunders allowed reporters into his woodwork shop. Reporters saw him in an uncharacteristic pose, sweaty, dressed in workingman's clothing and covered with sawdust. Saunders acknowledged to them that his appearance was far different from his celebrated past, yet he was proud of his productive work. "I like woodwork," he said, "I know it." Building wagons was not the work Saunders wanted to do: "I don't expect to make a fortune out of this. It's a living and something to keep me occupied until I can get back in the grocery business. You know, I can't keep idle. After the war, it's back to the grocery business for me, back to my Keedoozle, back to the top one last time."

He told them he had been constantly thinking of ways to improve the Keedoozle. The idea was sound, he still believed, but the mechanical problems were more numerous than he had first imagined. Soon he would have the Keedoozle perfected. Saunders revealed to them his thoughts about his career: "I can't say I've regretted a bit of it. If I could have kept my first millions I would be dead today—rotted away from inactivity. I've enjoyed building up and then, when my playhouse fell, starting again from scratch."

Like his father, Lee Saunders was always busy producing and selling a clever idea. During the war, he served on the War Manpower Commission. He opened his own manpower employment business. One of his partners in the business was a mechanical engineer, Woody Forbes. On their own time, he and Forbes designed a golf club putter, the "One-Putt," out of solid cast magnesium. Lee Saunders devised a means to compute the sales tax on a National Cash Register machine or a Burroughs cash register. He sold the procedure to a number of grocery stores until the National Cash Register Company purchased it from him. Subsequently, Lee Saunders invented a trading stamps dispenser that he sold to Kroger Grocery Company.

World War II ended on September 2, 1945, with the surrender of Japan. Clarence Saunders immediately set in motion his plans for Keedoozle. Within four months, he announced the new Keedoozle would be ready to demonstrate to the public. Saunders and his crew had devised a new printing system for the customer's receipt tape.

When the customer inserted the key with the adding machine tape at the tip into the desired slot, green and red lights flashed. Instantly, the type inside of the slot perforated a pattern of holes on the adding machine

Business Week described the pattern of holes as like "the contact holes on a key-punched tabulating card." Saunders estimated the system could trip twenty items in four seconds. *Courtesy of the Memphis Room, Memphis Public Library and Information Center.*

tape. It was this pattern of dots that now tripped the chute mechanisms to release the groceries down to the conveyor belt. The dots could be arranged to form 4,096 different combinations, with each combination a code representing a different item.

Saunders contracted the Automatic Electric Company of Chicago to build the demonstration model in that city. "It can't miss," he said. "It's my last big plunge, and it's by far the best thing that ever came along in the grocery business." *Newsweek* magazine was not confident that the idea could work: "Skeptics thought Saunders was playing with the world's biggest pinball machine and would never succeed in lighting all its lights." Others said, "They called Piggly Wiggly a pipe dream too."

Still the mechanical defects caused problems. During one test of the demonstration store in Chicago, a chute accidentally released cans of turnips on top of a news reporter. Saunders chartered, in July 1946, the Automatic Systems, Inc., with Lee Saunders and Victor Laughter as officers, to build the next Keedoozle in Memphis. Again optimistic, he claimed, "It is perfect now. There is no way for it to fail. We have spent eleven years and $600,000 taking all the bugs out of it. We will go all over the world with it. The largest grocery chain in Holland has already asked for the machinery to mechanize their stores."

Saunders wanted to sell the Keedoozle to other businesses in addition to retail grocers. He ventured that the Keedoozle mechanisms would be useful to warehouse businesses, mail-order houses, factories, drugstores and auto parts stores. Apparently only one Keedoozle system was ever sold, manufactured and delivered to another firm.

Attracting investment to Keedoozle was becoming increasingly difficult. In 1947, Lee Saunders told Woody Forbes, "You ought to go see Dad. He's still in there pecking and beating away. He hasn't got a quarter, hasn't got a dime."

Forbes visited Saunders at his office in the M and M Building on Main and Beale. Forbes gave him $100 and turned to leave, and Saunders said, "Wait, let me give you this." It was a stock certificate for his company, Automatic Systems, Inc. Forbes doubted Saunders would ever perfect the Keedoozle. He admired Saunders for his stubbornness, his determination to continue with the Keedoozle despite its problems. Forbes agreed to work part time on the Keedoozle project because of his friendship with Lee Saunders and his respect for Mr. Saunders.

Somehow, Clarence Saunders found the investment to build one last model of Keedoozle. In January 1948, he commissioned a Quonset hut roughly two stories tall for the new Keedoozle. The Quonset hut was a design used by the armed forces during World War II. It was a completely metal building with a roof shaped as an arch that "looked like a tin can sliced in half by its length." Saunders believed its design suited his needs well. The Quonset hut could be prefabricated at a shop and assembled easily on the site. All the Keedoozle franchise stores were to be Quonset huts.

He leased eight acres of land for his Keedoozle store near the Belt Line railroad at the corner of Poplar and Union Extended in the eastern suburbs of Memphis. Eventually, he promised to build a shopping village of Keedoozle warehouses and a variety of retail stores on the site. The first store carried only dry packaged goods and frozen foods.

The new Keedoozle was small, twenty feet by sixty feet, with an interior arrangement similar to his previous models. Saunders said then a single cashier could handle five customers a minute, a rate that could only be equaled by ten cashiers in an ordinary supermarket. He expected to operate the Keedoozle with one-fifth of the personnel a supermarket employed. Saunders purchased his merchandise in quantity, using his railroad access to ship carload lots to his Keedoozle. He then priced his merchandise one cent above the manufacturer's costs on all items costing more than ten cents, giving himself a slim profit margin. He predicted, as he had before with Keedoozle, great success: "It is a cinch, five years— five billion dollars."

Saunders opened the store on August 19, 1948, to an estimated crowd of six thousand. Conspicuous in his white flannel suit and trousers, which matched his white hair, Saunders hustled around the store filling orders at the cashier's desk and helping the inexperienced employees place sacks of groceries with the right customers. Old friends who had shopped in his Piggly Wiggly stores came by to congratulate him. He escorted *Press-Scimitar* reporter Clark Porteous on a tour of the store. He cheerfully tried his best to explain the complex mechanism to Porteous. The young reporter discovered Saunders's perverse sense of humor. He noticed a can of rattlesnake meat that was on display behind glass. "Oh! That's a delicacy," said the Keedoozle man. "Take some home and try it." "Ugh, No thank-you, Mr. Saunders."

Saunders again attracted some investors, presumably not with the rattlesnake meat. Joseph Levy, owner of a chain grocery store in Pittsburgh,

Saunders enjoyed showing off his store. Saunders led the Fischer family to the second floor. He asked Miss Leola Fischer to climb on the conveyor belt and slide down. She would not do that unless he slid down the belt first. And so he did, to the delight of his audience. *Courtesy of the Memphis Room, Memphis Public Library and Information Center.*

visited the Keedoozle store. He had purchased the franchise rights of Keedoozle for his city. Levy was excited about Saunders's innovation. The Keedoozle handled a greater volume of business than his largest ordinary store in Pittsburgh. In August, a reporter from *Time* magazine visited Saunders at his Keedoozle, twelve years after the magazine's first visit. The reporter wrote, "Customers liked the pinball type lights that danced as they inserted their keys. Better still they liked his prices that were 10% to 15% cheaper than the average store."

The Keedoozle machinery troubled Saunders more than price fixing. His crew had to change some of the chutes because certain odd-size grocery items did not fit properly. Shoppers complained that the new adding machines gave inaccurate information. Customers also demanded a greater variety of merchandise in the Keedoozle. He wanted to expand his machinery's ability to handle fresh meats, fruits and vegetables, but once again, he could

His cheap prices violated the Tennessee Fair Trade Law. This allowed manufacturers of the product and selected retailers to set retail prices, which were binding to all retailers. Saunders called it "the Price Gouging Law." *Courtesy of the Memphis Room, Memphis Public Library and Information Center.*

not. He added a conventional store arrangement for the perishable goods. Shoppers picked their own choices. He named this department the "Duck Waddle." In January 1949, Saunders was pleased to announce that certain investors were ready to open Keedoozles in the New York City area.

The high costs of maintenance and product breakage undoubtedly influenced businessmen not to invest in Keedoozle. Saunders quickly ran out of money to operate the store. Suppliers refused to extend him credit. He could no longer keep many grocery items in stock. In August 1949, one year after the store opened, Saunders asked the stockholders for more money, which they refused to provide. Weary of the Keedoozle, he closed the store on August 17 with this statement: "After 14 years I am finally fed up with gadgets. Keedoozle was too much for the average mind to comprehend. It was too far in advance of public thinking."

Saunders's financial problems had not ended. The Securities and Exchange Commission filed an injunction in federal court to stop Saunders and his company, Automatic Systems Corporation, from selling stock. Saunders settled out of court. He "donated" money from the Automatic Systems stock sale to the commission. He claimed the actual sale was so small that he was told he didn't have to report it to the government. His Automatic Systems Corporation then surrendered its property to the government for nonpayment of assessed taxes. The Keedoozle name was sold at auction sold for $1,250.

In 1950, the Piggly Wiggly Corporation held its franchise operators' convention in Memphis at the Peabody Hotel. A young executive of the company wanted to invite Clarence Saunders. The president of Piggly Wiggly refused. He feared Saunders would still harbor a grudge against Piggly Wiggly and disrupt the convention. Saunders reportedly was curious about the convention, inquiring about who would attend.

After the disposal of the Keedoozle, many people assumed Clarence Saunders, almost sixty-nine years old, was finished. He did receive an honor for his accomplishments, from an unexpected source. The Swedish Inventors Association inducted him as a member in 1949. Patricia and Ann accepted the award in Sweden on his behalf.

The *Press-Scimitar* asked reporter Robert Johnson to accompany Saunders on a tour of the Pink Palace Museum. Johnson asked him about the Piggly Wiggly stock market corner. Saunders talked again of how the New York Stock Exchange suspended its own rules to deprive him of his victory over member stockbrokers. "If it worked out the other way, I would have cleared about $40,000,000." He did not indulge in pathos for long. "It was just a day's work. Just a day's loss. I don't pine over it. I never regret. I've got too much to look forward to."

Saunders was busy thinking of ideas for his automatic grocery store. "I can't help it," he later said to the *Chicago Tribune*. "My mind keeps pumping, pumping, pumping…" He was trying to discover how to entice people into accepting automatic shopping. The mechanical breakdowns of the Keedoozle were an obvious frustration to the shoppers. He accepted grudgingly that the complexity of the machinery itself discouraged habitual use by shoppers. Saunders bitterly spoke of customers' reactions to the Keedoozle: "They were entranced. They were mystified. But that was not good business for the store. What we had was a free circus."

"Housewives did not care to 'fool' with it," an observer of the Keedoozle noted. "They preferred to take things off the shelf, look them over and keep it or leave it." Saunders now understood his task for the automatic store. He had to give to his customers complete mastery over the machines.

At the front entrance of the museum they admired his creation. "I guess it will be here as long as the pyramids are standing," Saunders mused. *Courtesy of the Memphis Room, Memphis Public Library and Information Center.*

He called the new store "Foodelectric." He and his crew devised a new key or gadget, a 3- by 1¼-inch metal rectangle roughly described as "a pistol shaped like a hammer." Inside the rectangle was a tiny "adding machine" that worked something like a counter with four rows of figures from 0 to 9. The adding machine was designed to let the customers total their purchase instead of the cashier.

Upon entering the store, the customer was to receive the new key, a shopping cart and paper sacks. The key gadget was to release the grocery items from the display case into an adjacent chute, like a vending machine. The customers were to pick the items from the chute and place them in their shopping cart. The cashier would look at the amount totaled on the counter and collect from shoppers, then run back the counter to zero. Saunders had not solved the riddle of how to sell refrigerated foods, fresh vegetables and meats in an automated store. He proposed substituting a proxy item, a wooden block, in the display chutes that the cashier would exchange for the correct item.

Again Lee diligently worked for his father, but not without protest from Mary Saunders. Over the years, she had watched father and son work hard building their dream store. Sometimes they would have money; often they would not. Lee was never sure when he would earn any income. Mary Saunders was not accustomed to the month-by-month worry of paying bills, and she relied upon her family's wealth to maintain a suitable lifestyle. When their business failed, Lee would quickly find a decent job. Then, his father would beckon again, and he would give up that security. She dreaded his summons.

Saunders's deteriorating health prevented his last comeback bid. He could not work and accomplish things as he once had done, which aggravated him. Saunders's temperament became more erratic and explosive during the last three years of his life. He was a frequent patient at the Wallace Sanitarium, a private hospital for those suffering emotional or mental illnesses. He insisted throughout that he would complete his work. In July 1953, Saunders let it be known that his Foodelectric was nearly complete and he would announce a grand opening in the near future. He expected to sell franchises in Foodelectric. He was, he said, on his way back to wealth.

His announcements for the Foodelectric were his last brave front. In the fall of 1953, he pushed himself to finish the Foodelectric. Saunders collapsed from exhaustion and was admitted again to the sanitarium. He died there on October 14, 1953.

Eldon Roark, in his column the next day, paid tribute to his friend Clarence Saunders: "His inventiveness was matched by only one thing, his indomitable persistence. Life was just too short for him."

His emotional turmoil at the end was the result of a fear that he would die a failure. Saunders had failed to achieve the third business empire that he had struggled for during the last twenty years of his life. He left behind no fortune, only a small amount of money and some personal belongings. His Foodelectric remained an unfinished idea.

Always fascinated with new technology, Saunders had reshaped his innovation, the self-service store arrangement, with automation. His last ideas were beyond the technology available to him. From the vantage point of sixty and seventy years later, it is remarkable that he tried to build the Keedoozle without the microchip or even the transistor. His stepson, Tunkie, was philosophical: "He should have stayed with the supermarkets. But he gambled…attempted new ideas. Pioneers, innovators [like him] often end up with nothing."

Roark contemplated this judgment of Clarence Saunders nine years after his death: "Some men achieve lasting fame through success, others achieve it through failure. And that's the way it was with the late Clarence Saunders." Roark liked to escort people new to Memphis on tours of the city. He would drive east on Central through the residential neighborhoods without informing them of his destination. Then they came upon the magnificent Pink Palace. His riders were always astonished by its commanding presence. He would tell them Clarence Saunders's story and how his home was now one of the city's cultural attractions: "Because he failed to lick Wall Street, in a terrific stock market battle in 1923, his story is told everyday in Memphis and people enjoy the fruits of his labor, the Pink Palace Museum."

In 1983, the Memphis Park Commission opened a nature center on a sixty-five-acre portion of the Annswood estate. The land was now enclosed by the city's eastern business district. The Park Commission constructed hiking trails around Saunders's lake, through the woods and pasture. They named the park after the Lichterman family, who had last owned the land and then donated it to the Park Commission. Clarence Saunders's log cabin home served as the Lichterman Nature Center headquarters until fire destroyed it in 1994.

Annswood and the Pink Palace inspired Ernie Pyle to say in 1936, "If Saunders lives long enough Memphis will become the most beautiful city in the world just with the things Saunders built and lost." Both of these cultural attractions are appropriate memorials to the life of Clarence Saunders.

The most fitting memorial to him is the ordinary self-service store. Sam Walton founded Wal-Mart in 1962. By the end of his life, in 1992, Walton owned the largest retail merchandising company in the world. In his autobiography, *Sam Walton Made in America*, he credited the enormous success of his retail stores to the principle of self-service. His brief description of the benefits that self-service gave to him and his desire to pass on the savings to his customers seemed to be a near match to Saunders's own words two generations before. During the past twenty-five years, supermarkets and the large merchandise stores have become popular in nearly every country in Europe, Asia, Latin America and parts of Africa. In an odd way, Clarence Saunders's prophetic slogan for Piggly Wiggly, "All Over the World," has come true.

ABOUT THE AUTHOR

For over thirty years, Mike Freeman has made a career out of his love for Memphis and regional history. He co-wrote, with Cindy Hazen, two books about Elvis Presley—*The Best of Elvis* in 1992 and *Memphis Elvis Style* in 1997—and a book based upon Patsy Cline's letters, *Love Always Patsy, Patsy Cline's Letters to a Friend*, in 1999. For eight years he owned and lived in the first home Elvis purchased at 1034 Audubon Drive in Memphis. Mike has also written or co-written magazine articles about the area's fascinating personalities. In 2007, Mike helped create three DVDs: *Elvis' Memphis* and *Beyond Elvis' Memphis* with Artsmagic, Inc. (UK) and *Elvis: Return to Tupelo* with Michael Rose Productions.

With his partner, Sue Mack, Mike continues to do research today and offers guided tours of the region. This biography of Clarence Saunders was actually his first project and his MA thesis. Until now, only excerpts of this work were published in the *Tennessee Historical Quarterly* (1992) and *Tennessee Encyclopedia* (1997).

Visit us at
www.historypress.net